Website Design

How to Build Websites That Work on Any Browser

(The Essential Guide to Typography for Print and Web Design)

Beverly Carrier

Published By **Zoe Lawson**

Beverly Carrier

Website Design: How to Build Websites That Work on Any Browser (The Essential Guide to Typography for Print and Web Design)

ISBN 978-1-77485-786-1

Legal & Disclaimer

The information contained in this ebook is not designed to replace or take the place of any form of medicine or professional medical advice. The information in this ebook has been provided for educational & entertainment purposes only.

The information contained in this book has been compiled from sources deemed reliable, and it is accurate to the best of the Author's knowledge; however, the Author cannot guarantee its accuracy and validity and cannot be held liable for any errors or omissions. Changes are periodically made to this book. You must consult your doctor or get professional medical advice before using any of the suggested remedies, techniques, or information in this book.

Upon using the information contained in this book, you agree to hold harmless the Author from and against any damages, costs, and expenses, including any legal fees potentially resulting from the application of any of the information provided by this guide. This disclaimer applies to any damages or injury caused by the use and application, whether directly or indirectly, of any advice or information presented, whether for breach of contract, tort, negligence, personal injury, criminal intent, or under any other cause of action.

You agree to accept all risks of using the information presented inside this book. You need to consult a professional medical practitioner in order to ensure you are both able and healthy enough to participate in this program.

TABLE OF CONTENTS

Introduction

This section is the building block for all upcoming sections. It explains how and why websites were introduced. It also throws light upon the connection of different frontend technologies with website development.

Chapter 1: Website Development

If you have worked upon Frontend development, then you must know that a browser mainly understands HTML (Hypertext Mark-up Language) tags. These tags are beautified using a language called CSS (Cascading Style Sheets). The controls of a website are managed by scripting languages (like JavaScript). In case you don't know these, then no worries, we are going to discuss these concepts in detail later.

1.2 Learning Path

To keep the learning in a continuum, we will start from very basic that includes Internet basics, how a browser works, individual learnings for HTML, CSS and JavaScript, XML libraries and JSON. Once we have a better understanding of these concepts, then we can develop our websites independently.

The above topics are mentioned not to panic you but to give an overview of what will you learn after completing this guide book. After completing this book, you will become a website developer.

2. Internet Basics

In this section, we will be discussing mainly these things: What is a protocol, what the Internet is, how the internet works and how the website works. These are the concepts which every frontend developer should know.

2.1 What is a protocol

How do we communicate? We use different languages for communication. I am an Indian and suppose my client is a German. In our case, I speak Hindi, and he speaks German. Now, there is a communication gap/barrier.

To eliminate this barrier, we use a common language to communicate which is English. There is one mandatory prerequisite, which is, both of us must understand English and our English must be the same (same 26 alphabets). It sounds funny that I am saying that our English should be the same. What if, we both have different versions of the English language, then also there will be a communication gap/barrier. Thus, the whole world has the same version of the English language. This global acceptability of a language is termed as a protocol in networking.

A protocol in a communication network is a set of rules and guidelines used for communicating data. These rules are defined for each step and process that occurs during communication between two or more computers. Networks must follow these rules to successfully transmit data across servers or computers.

Now, you know what a protocol is. But how a protocol is executed and understood by our browsers. A browser is developed in such a way that it understands HTTP and other protocols. Even you might have seen https:// or http:// in your browser. These protocols have to be implemented in a specific way while coding. We will discuss the HTTP and HTTPS protocols implementation later. Apart from these website protocols, the basic protocol for internet is TCP/IP.

TCP/IP stands for Transmission Control Protocol/Internet Protocol, and it is implemented on an operating system. Every operating system has these protocols pre-implemented. Once your website is on the Internet, and your browser tries to connect to your website, TCP/IP is automatically executed, to run it. The definition of these protocols is defined by World Wide Web Consortium, which is the main international standards organisation for the World Wide Web (W3) or WWW.

We have discussed protocols just because they will be mentioned in topics later. Now, you might have some idea about a protocol and its importance.

2.2. What is an Internet

The internet of now was developed as a pilot project under the United States Department of Defence and was called ARPANET. Around 1995, it was brought to the public and operated by the commercial internet service providers.

In general terms, it is called a network of networks. The Internet has become an essential part of our day to day life. From sending mails, browsing the web to downloading files,

everything takes just a blink of an eye. This is possible due to its peer-to-peer mesh network.
The internet is a network which uses TCP/IP (protocols) to transmit data via various media such as wireless, fibre optic, etc. An internet connects various computers and servers using a communication medium.

2.3. How the Internet works

As discussed above, the internet is a network accessed via wire (fibre optic) or wireless. Internet is useful because any two computers directly connected to internet wire (network) can communicate. A server is a special computer that is connected directly to the internet. All the web pages and web data are stored on the hard drives of these servers. Every server has a unique internet protocol address or IP address. Just like a postal address, IP address helps computers to find each other. The IP addresses are a set of numbers which are hard to remember for every website. That's why we give them a name (or Domain Name System) as google.com or gocoding.org.
Your computer at home is not a server as it is not connected directly with the internet. These computers are termed as clients. To connect to the internet, clients (our computers) use Internet Service Provider or ISP (the company that is providing you the internet service).
Scenario 1:

Let's assume; I want to mail a text message to one of my friends, Aditya. I have an account of Gmail, and my friend uses Outlook.

I will log on to Gmail.com and compose a message to my friend's email address. Once I click send, Gmail server will send the email to Outlook server.

The next day, when my friend Aditya will log on to Outlook server, then he will retrieve the email.

Whenever an email, picture or a webpage travels across the internet, computers break the information into smaller pieces called packets.

When the information reaches the destination, the package is reassembled in original order to generate a picture, email, webpage or tweet.

Scenario 2:

Imagine you are at work, sitting next to your boss and you both are surfing online. Your boss is doing market research, and you are updating your Tinder profile. You both are sending packets back and forth over the internet. What will happen if your packet accidently reaches your boss' screen? That could be embarrassing.

The solution to that problem is IP addresses and routers. Everything connected directly or indirectly through the internet has an IP address. It includes your mobile phones, your computers, Wi-Fi routers and everything. Wherever two or more parts of the internet intersects, a router is placed there. Routers direct our package around the internet helping each package get one step closer to its destination. Every time you visit a website, up to ten to fifteen routers may help your packets find their way to and from your computer. Each time a data leaves a device, its IP address is added to the packet. Each time a packet reaches a new router, another layer is added until it reaches the required server. Then, when the server sends back the information, it creates a package with identical wrapping. As the package makes its way over the internet back to your computer. Each wrapper unwraps the layer to discover where to send the package next until it reaches your computer and not your boss's. And, that's how the internet works.

2.4 How the Website works

We have already discussed, how the internet works. Now, using the internet, we display our websites to the end user. It is very important to know how a website gets loaded into a browser. This will not only help you to write better codes but will also help you to debug your code efficiently.

To understand how a website works, we will discuss the client-server concept, website component files, how the browser works, and the DOM tree.

2.4.1 Clients and Servers

As discussed earlier, there are two types of computers connected to the internet, called clients and servers. A simplified diagram of how a server and a client communicate with each other is shown below:

- Servers are the devices that are directly connected to the internet and are used to store webpages, sites, apps and files. Whenever a user opens a website, it is downloaded from these servers.
- Clients are the devices that are used by a user, i.e. our personal computers, mobiles, tablets, etc. These devices have web browsing software pre-installed in it (i.e. browsers like chrome or Firefox).

2.4.2 Website Component Files

A website is made up of different types of files. These files can be categorised into two sections:

- Code Files: All the websites are built primarily from HTML, CSS and JavaScript. Although you might have seen other technologies being involved in websites development. These files too, are later rendered and converted into these primary languages itself.
- Assets: All other stuff that makes a website apart from primary language files comes into assets, i.e. images, music, video, pdfs, etc.

2.4.3 How Browser Works

The main functionality of a browser is to present the website you choose, by requesting it from the respective server and displaying it in the browser. In given subtopic, we will discuss the structure and functionality of major browsers, i.e. Chrome, Internet Explorer and Firefox.

A browser's high-level structure includes the following:

- User Interface: Everything that you can see on a browser, i.e. address bar, buttons, display window, etc.
- Rendering Engine: It parses HTML, XML, CSS, etc.; and displays the content accordingly on the screen.
- Networking: It performs all the network call requests, e.g. HTTP requests.
- JavaScript Interpreter: It parses and executes the JavaScript codes.
- Data storage: Every browser supports persistence layer data storage. It means, you can store your data locally on the browser as cache and it never gets deleted until the browser cache is cleared. We will later utilise this browser feature in our codes too.

Apart from the components mentioned above, there are other components that are not relevant to this guide book.

2.4.4 DOM: Document Object Model

DOM is a cross platform programming interface that treats HTML, XML and other mark-up languages in the form of a tree structure. In a DOM every tag/element is represented by an individual node. Every browser utilises a DOM structure to display a webpage.

Once the browser gets the content of a webpage from the server, it parses the XML into HTML and later converts the element of HTML to DOM nodes in a tree called "content tree". Then the CSS is parsed and converted into a tree called "render tree". The nodes of these trees are later displayed on the screen according to their coordinates. A generic example is shown below:

Figure 1 HTML DOM Tree Diagram

The learning point here is that, whatever code you write for frontend, it will be converted into the basic languages, i.e. HTML, CSS and JavaScript. And the HTML and CSS will be converted into a DOM tree structure and will be then displayed on the browser window accordingly.

3. How professionals do coding?

Before we start with the web development, we need to know the correct approach for web development. We will now discuss the mandatory steps, before starting the web development, which is recommended by professionals.

What tools to use?

Every coding needs some pre-requisite configurations and tools to run. For HTML, we need the following set-ups:

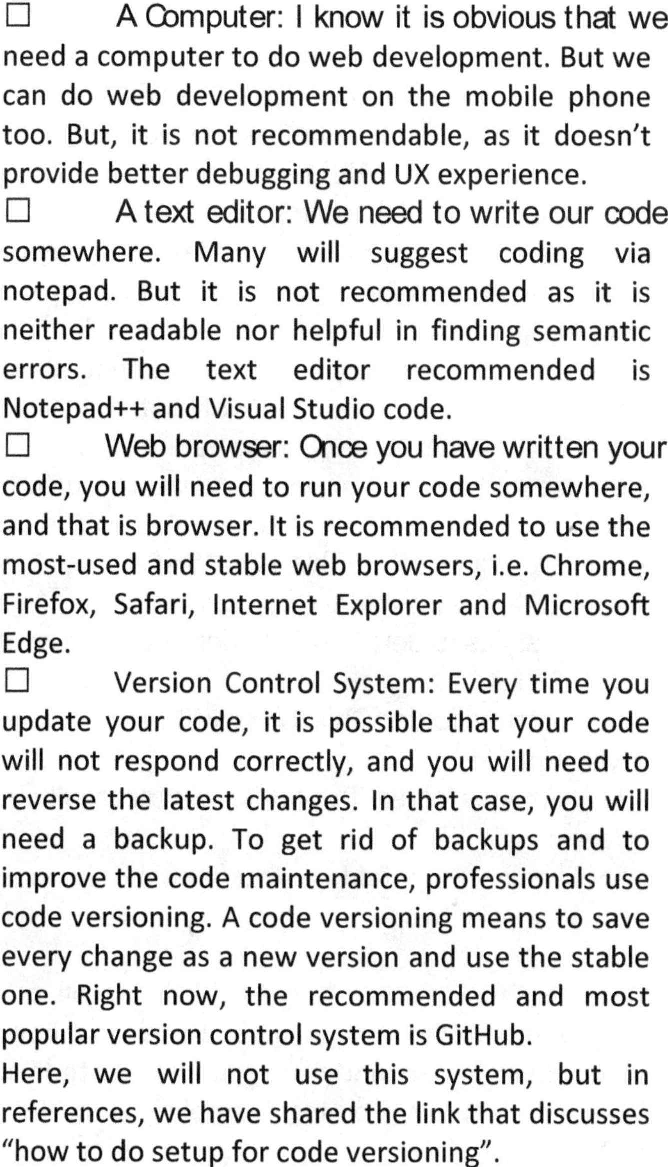

□ A Computer: I know it is obvious that we need a computer to do web development. But we can do web development on the mobile phone too. But, it is not recommendable, as it doesn't provide better debugging and UX experience.

□ A text editor: We need to write our code somewhere. Many will suggest coding via notepad. But it is not recommended as it is neither readable nor helpful in finding semantic errors. The text editor recommended is Notepad++ and Visual Studio code.

□ Web browser: Once you have written your code, you will need to run your code somewhere, and that is browser. It is recommended to use the most-used and stable web browsers, i.e. Chrome, Firefox, Safari, Internet Explorer and Microsoft Edge.

□ Version Control System: Every time you update your code, it is possible that your code will not respond correctly, and you will need to reverse the latest changes. In that case, you will need a backup. To get rid of backups and to improve the code maintenance, professionals use code versioning. A code versioning means to save every change as a new version and use the stable one. Right now, the recommended and most popular version control system is GitHub.

Here, we will not use this system, but in references, we have shared the link that discusses "how to do setup for code versioning".

There are more tools that are used by professionals for development and testing, we will discuss others later as per the need.

What structure should your website have?

A website consists of different types of files: html code file (.html file), styling code file (.css file), scripting file (like .js file), media files (like images) and many more. When the project gets bigger, it becomes important to organize these files in their separate folders. Also, it is recommended to name them in lower case and without any space (dash "-" or underscore "_" may be used).

Now let us have a look on the structure of our website:

- ☐ index.html: This is the first file that is searched and executed by a browser
- ☐ styles folder: In this folder we will keep all our CSS files.
- ☐ scripts folder: This folder will contain all our JavaScript files.
- ☐ images folder: This folder will contain all our images.

As of now, your folder structure should look something like this:

Here test-form is the folder which has all our development files and folders. Once you have made these folders and files, open index.html file in notepad++. In upcoming examples, we will be just coding in HTML.

What will your website look like?

This is the most important question every developer must ask to self. To answer this, you need to answer following:

- ☐ What exactly your website is all about?
- ☐ What are the functionalities you want from your website?
- ☐ What are the content you want to display on your website?
- ☐ How your website will look?

I will take a scenario to answer all the above questions. These answers will vary person-to-person and according to the requirement. I will also discuss tools to use, that will help you in all above cases.

Scenario: Registration form for Social Networking site (e.g. Gmail)

What exactly your website is all about?

☐ It is a mailing website which needs a registration form to be filled.

What are the functionalities you want from your website?

☐ Give input boxes to take inputs and a button to show a popup with successful message.

What are the content you want to display on your website?

☐ I want to display my website name in bold letters, an image, instructions for username and password.

How your website will look?

□ For this either I will draw my layout on paper or use an online tool like Balsamiq.

UX design using Pen-Paper
It means, I will draw my exact UI design for all the pages. For given scenario, we can draw something like this:

UX design using any online tool (e.g. Balsamiq)
Online tools provide drag and drop option to create a UI design. For given scenario, we can draw something like this:

From above planning, we will understand what and where exactly we have to write our code. Here, I will use HTML to create all the UI design, CSS to provide colour and style to it and JavaScript to perform pop up operation on button click.

4. Hypertext Markup Language (HTML)

HTML is a Markup language that is used to define the structure of your content on a website with the help of a browser. A Markup language is a computer language which uses tags to define elements in a document. These elements can be a paragraph, image, bullet points, tables or anything that you see daily in your word or paper documents.

The tags that encloses a word can change the way it behaves. It can be easily understood from the examples below:

Case 1:
Here, we have just used <p> tags (paragraph tags) as shown below in our code:

When we run this code on browser, we get given output:

Note: Try these examples by your own. Open the index.html file we have created earlier in notepad++ and test it by opening the same in a browser.
Case 2:
Here, we have used <a> tags (anchor tags) as shown below in our code:

When we run this code on browser, we get given output:

In the above screen, the term “Google” is a link which redirects to http://www.google.com on click.
Case 3:
Here, we have used <h1> tags (Heading 1 tag) as shown below in our code:

When we run this code on browser, we get given output:

From above examples, we can derive that a HTML tag includes the following:

1. The opening tag: This tag consists of a tag name enclosed between angle brackets <> and marks the opening of a tag i.e. from where the effect of the tag will start.
2. The closing tag: Just like the opening tag, this tag also consists of a tag name but preceded by a forward slash "/", all enclosed between angle brackets <>. This marks the closing of a tag i.e. from where the effect of the tag will end.
3. The content: This is the content that is actually visible on the browser
4. The element: The opening tag, the content and the closing tag together make an element.

Attribute of an Element

The elements discussed above can also have its own properties called attributes. An attribute of an element contains extra information regarding it and is not displayed with the actual content. In the above cases you have seen <a> tag with href attribute. These attributes enhance the features of an element. This can be easily understood by below examples:

Example 1: Image tag consists of an attribute src which specifies the source of the image.

Code:

Output:

Example 2: We can use attribute to fix height and width of an image too.

Code:

Note: Every tag must be closed so that it doesn't affect other tags. Some tags are empty elements i.e. it doesn't have separate opening and closing tags, e.g. <Image/> tag, hence it has no content to be shown apart from the image fetched from the source.

Output:

From above examples, we can derive that an attribute includes the following:

1. A space: A space between the element tag name and an attribute or between two attributes.
2. The attribute name: These are predefined for each html tags. These are followed by an equal to sign "=".
3. The attribute value: These are the values assigned to the attribute names. These are wrapped within quotation marks " ".

Nested Elements

All the examples we have discussed above had one tag. Now, let's assume, you have a requirement to show some texts of a sentence in bold and others as simple text. This can be achieved using nested elements. This can be easily understood by given example:

Example:

In this code, we have used two tags <p> and <b>.

Note: HTML tags are not case sensitive. Thus, <b> and <B> will behave in the same way.
Output:

Anatomy of an HTML document
When we develop a website and publish it on a web server, the website can be accessed via its URL e.g. www.w3schools.com. Now, when we try to open this website, by default it loads index.html and it is the name used as homepage of the website.

You can see many things are written in that index page. Among them, we will discuss only the HTML tags below:

From above example, we can derive that an HTML page includes the following:

- <!DOCTYPE html>: The <!DOCTYPE> declaration is not an HTML tag. It is an instruction to the web browser regarding the version of HTML, the page is written in. Therefore, it must be the very first thing in your HTML document. <!DOCTYPE html> declaration is for HTML5.
- <html></html>: The <html> tag represents the root of an HTML document, and you can refer DOM discussed above for the same. The <html> tag tells the browser that the page that is loading is an HTML document.

- <head></head>: This is the area where we put all those stuffs that will be not visible as a content of our webpage. This includes: CSS source, script source, meta tags, etc.
- <meta http-equiv="X-UA-Compatible" content="IE=edge" />: If your webpage supports Internet Explorer or not, this is specified using X-UA-Compatible and the version is defined in content, here it is IE=edge.
- <meta charset="utf-8">: UTF-8 is an encoding methodology which includes characters of almost every written language. Since, browser understands English only, it is important to use Unicode UTF-8 to tell the meaning of a character to our browser.
- <title></title>: It is used to set title of our webpage and it appears in the browser tab. You can see "Google Mail Signup" appearing in browser tab in the picture below.
- <body></body>: It is used to show all the content to our webpage users and it includes texts, images, videos, audios and everything else.

The above code will produce given output:

Important tags in HTML

Tag Description Example

<img> It is used to add Image <img src="your_image_source">

<h1>-<h6> It is used to add heading <h1>Your main title</h1>

<h2>Your top-level heading</h2>

<h3>Your subheading</h3>
<h4>Your sub-subheading</h4>

<p> It is used to add paragraph <p> Add your paragraph here </p>

<a> It is used to add link <a href="your_link>Text to be clicked</a>

<div> It is used to add a division or a section <div> Other HTML elements </div>

 It is used to add a line break

Chapter 2: Lists In Html

In HTML, we have two types of Lists: Unordered and Ordered List.

The list points within any of these lists are mentioned within <li></li>.

Unordered List

Many times, it is required to print some bullet points within a paragraph. These bullet points are called an unordered list in HTML. This can be easily understood by given syntax and example:

Syntax

Example

Output

Ordered List

The above mentioned list can also be displayed in numbers in place of bullets. These numbers will be in order and hence termed as an ordered list in HTML.

Syntax:

Example

Output

Tables in HTML

In real world applications, tables are widely used to display organization data. To display table in HTML we use <table> tag. For each row we use <tr> tag [tr stands for table row] and for each header and column we use <th> [table header] and <td> [table data] tag respectively. This can be easily understood by given syntax and example:

Syntax

Example

Output

Note: You might be missing table border here. Table border comes under CSS section, which will be covered later.

Forms in HTML

You might have filled a lot of forms in your life, offline and online. To sign up at any website, we need to fill a form with our basic details. These form data are later saved in a database table. Every time, you try to login, your data is fetched from the same table. HTML too provides tags to develop an online form.

Within form too, we need different types of controls like: we need to take input text for name, radio button for gender, checkboxes for subjects, calendar for date of birth, submit button etc.

Note: A form itself is never visible, it integrates multiple elements all together and performs a single action on them.

Syntax

Example

Output

HTML Exercise

HTML, in itself, is a huge topic. If you have understood till here, then we will do a simple exercise using HTML tags.

Exercise 1: Develop a website as shown in the picture below:

Code:

Exercise 2: Develop a website as shown in the picture below:

Note: We have not provided code for this example. You need to write the code by yourself. The image of Kung Fu Panda shown above is default hardcoded image added using image tag and not searched via internet.

5. Cascading Style Sheets (CSS)

Once, we have learnt HTML coding, it becomes important to learn CSS. CSS helps us to beautify our HTML output. With CSS you can add colours, change width and height, add spacing, fix position of your element, and add background images and everything else that you think can make your output screen beautiful.

A CSS is neither a programming language nor a Markup language but a styling sheet language. A styling sheet language helps us to add styles into our document/output.

We have already made a folder “styles” under the structure section above. In that folder, create a text/notepad file and save it naming “style.css”. And this type of CSS is known as External CSS. We can add CSS into HTML file itself altogether which is known as Internal CSS. You can even add CSS directly into the HTML element which is known as Inline CSS. To better understand them, let’s discuss all one by one.

Type of CSS

As discussed above, CSS can be added into our website in following three ways:

- External CSS (In a separate file)
- Internal CSS (At the top of a web page document)
- Inline CSS (Right next to the text it decorates)

External CSS

As discussed above, we have already created a file with name “style.css” in folder “styles”. But, our HTML file i.e. index.html doesn’t know its location. Therefore, we need to add given code in the header section [between <head> and </head>] of our HTML file:

```
<LINK HREF="STYLES/STYLE.CSS" REL="STYLESHEET" TYPE="TEXT/CSS">
```

Example:

As of now, we have just added the location of CSS file but no code into our CSS file. Thus, the output looks something like this:

Now we will add codes into our CSS file. We will make the Header Red, Sub Header Blue and the paragraph Green as mentioned below:

Now, the output looks something like this:

From above example, we can derive that a CSS code includes following:

1. Selector: A selector helps us to know exactly for which element we want to add a given style. In the diagram above, we are applying green colour for all the <p> tags. This type of selector is called Element selector [also known as tag or type selector]. If you need to style a different element, say <h1>, just change the selector name in CSS.

There are many types of selectors. Following are the three mostly used selectors:

Selector name Description Example
1. Element selector Under this category, we define a common style for an individual html tag and it reflects same style for that tag, wherever it is used. p {
 color: green;
}

This will reflect green colour for all the p tags.

2. ID selector Under this category, we give ID to any html tag, and for that ID we define a style. Same ID cannot be assigned to multiple HTML tags; hence it is mostly used in case unique style is needed for a specific HTML element.

In CSS, we define it using hash-symbol (#). CSS:

```
#my-id1 {
  color: green;
}
```

HTML:

```
<p id="my-id1">
```

This will reflect green colour for any html tag which has ID equal to "my-id1".

3. Class selector Under this category, we define a class for any html tag, and for that class we define a style. It is the most used CSS selector because same class can be assigned to multiple html tags, hence a CSS style can be reused.

In CSS, we define it using a dot(.). CSS:

```
.my-class {
  color: green;
}
```

HTML:

```
<p class="my-class1">
```

This will reflect green colour for any html tag which has class equal to "my-class1".

2. Declaration: A declaration is a field value pair, where field is one of the element properties

that you want to change, and the value is the required change. E.g. color: red;

3. Property: As discussed above, property is the attribute of an element which can be modified. Possible attributes for paragraph tag i.e. <p> can be color, alignment, font, etc.

4. Property Value: This is the possible value for a property and changes accordingly. For color, it can be any colour in Hexadecimal or colour name.

Important points regarding CSS declaration:

- The whole structure of a CSS is called a rule or rule set. Each rule set must be declared within curly braces ({ }).
- Each Declaration must be in the form of a field: value or Property: Property value pair i.e. it must have a colon (:) between field and value.
- Within each rule set, we can have multiple declaration. Each declaration must be terminated or separated from one another via semicolon (;).

Internal CSS

In above examples, we have used an external CSS file to place our styling code, but you can also add all these codes altogether with HTML code. For that, you need to add CSS under <style> </style> within the header section [between <head> and </head>] of HTML. This can be better understood from given example:

Syntax:

Example:

We will take our old example of Sachin Tendulkar. We will remove the link between External CSS and add same CSS within our HTML code:

Output: Here, we have just added an extra CSS declaration for <p> tag and made it bold. Thus, the output looks something like this:

Inline CSS

Suppose, you have applied CSS for all <p> tags, and there is a need to add unique style for one of the <p> tag, then you will have to use Inline CSS. An Inline CSS is used to add unique style to a single element.

To use inline style, we add "style" as an attribute of that element.

Syntax:

<tag_name style= "<Relevant Style Code>">
</tag_name>

Example: In the previous example, we will just add one inline style with internal CSS.

Output: Thus, the output will be as shown below:

From above example, we can also conclude that an Inline CSS can override another type of CSS. Thus, the priority of CSS that will be followed by the webpage will be as follow:

1. Inline Style (Highest Priority)
2. External and Internal Style (they have nearly same priority)

3. Browser's Default (Even browser apply CSS to our elements)

CSS layout

It is very important to understand CSS layout as it helps us to put a border around our content and manage its position and spacing with respect to the output screen. Each of our html element has the following CSS properties regarding layout:

- Border: As the name suggests, it is the solid line just outside your element. To better understand these concepts, I have turned the background colour of the body of our previous example as black.

Now, we will add CSS to enable border:

Note: From now onwards, we will be just taking example of External CSS

Output:

- Padding: In the above example, you can see that the texts are too close to the border, hence we need to add some space between the border and the content. These spaces are called padding. Padding are added to the content for which spacing is required. This will be clearer with the below example:

Example:

In the above example, we have added padding for all the content tags i.e. <h1>, <h2> and <p>. Here,

we have just used padding-left, which adds space only at the left side of the content. Just adding padding will add spaces all around the content, which we didn't want here.
Output:

- Margin: Unlike padding, it adds spacing outside an element with respect to the UI screen. In the above example, if we need to add spacing in left side of the border, then it will be a margin. This will be clearer from the given example:
Example:

In the above code, we have added margin just outside the border, and the border is made for <div> tag here. We have added margin only to the left side and it is 30% of the total width of the screen. It will bring the content somewhere in the middle of the screen as shown below:

CSS Layout Overview
If we merge the margin, the border and the padding altogether for an element, then it will look something like below image:

Chapter 3: Browser Based Css Debugging

If you go to your browser and open the "Inspect" portion, by right clicking mouse on the browser, you will land up on a section shown below. Here under "Elements" tab, you will find both of your HTML and CSS codes.

Just use this button to hover and select any element on UI for which you want to see/modify CSS.

In our case, we will be modifying our sub header. Thus, we will select "The God of Cricket" using the above-mentioned button. Once, we click it, we will get given screen:

What we found that whatever CSS code we wrote for <h2> tag is getting reflected here. Now, you can just add code directly here. These codes will be applicable only for current instance of webpage and gets restored to the old code, once refreshed. So, once you have got what you wanted in terms of style, you need to paste the same code in our CSS code file.

Here, we have just changed the colour and font-style to italic for H2 tag and the same is reflected in the output screen:

CSS Exercise

We are now aware of both HTML and CSS coding paradigm. Now, we can go back to our very first assignment (Registration form for Social Networking site) and try to develop it.

6. eXtensible Markup Language (XML)

We have earlier discussed HTML, which is a W3C standard markup language. HTML tags are predefined, and we can add custom tags in HTML. But what, if you want your whole markup language to be custom one such that it is capable of sending, receiving, storing and displaying data. In that case, we go for XML.

In reality, XML does not do anything by itself. It is just an information wrapped within tags. XML tags are not predefined and, therefore, needs someone to define meaning of its each tag.

Points to remember:

- XML documents are just like HTML and thus have element trees with a root element.

This can be understood with an example of table.

- All XML must have a closing tag (as shown in above examples)
- XML tags are case sensitive (Column and column are different tags in XML)

- XML elements must be properly nested (It means, you cannot have </columns> tag before </Column> tag)
- XML attribute values must always be quoted (In above example, “Column1” is an attribute value and is quoted)
- You cannot insert some characters in XML. To use these characters, you will have to use their alternate names. Following are the characters with their alternatives:

Character (Description)	Alternative to be used in XML
< (Less than)	<
> (Greater than)	>
& (Ampersand)	&
‘ (Apostrophe)	'
“ (Quotation mark)	"

- The syntax for adding comments in XML is similar to that of HTML (<!-- This is a comment -->)
- White spaces in XML are preserved and not ignored (The text is displayed with the white spaces added initially)
- XML uses prefix to avoid name conflict

□If you have multiple XML libraries, how will you differentiate among the origin of that tag. To solve this issue, we use a prefix before every tag and that prefix is defined at the beginning of the XML. It will be clear from given example:

Here we have used two different libraries: sap.m and sap.ui.layout and hence gave them the namespace as m and l.

Default Namespace: You can make one of your namespace as default. Suppose, we make sap.m as default library. In that case, we will not give it any namespace and also none of the tags that comes under sap.m library will carry namespace 'm'. The same thing is implemented in the code below:

XML Parser

Many times, there is a requirement to parse XML response. By parsing, we mean taking out the required information from a bunch of coded data. In this situation, we will already have the XML response in a variable. In the syntax and examples given below, we will parse required data from an XML code.

Syntax:

If you already have your XML data in a variable e.g. input.

Then, to parse we will write given code:

```
parser = new DOMParser();
xmlDoc =
parser.parseFromString(input,"text/xml");
```

Example:

In the example mentioned above, we have the XML code in our variable “input”. That is then parsed (or accessed) into another variable “xmlDoc”. Later, we have picked the title of the book from XML. This code was written in console of browser (press F12 to open console). These codes are written in JavaScript which will be discussed later.

The output is highlighted above.

XML Validator

We have already discussed that an XML should have code written in such a way that each tag is closed at correct position. Sometimes, we forget to close a tag and if the length of the code is too long, then it becomes tedious to find out the missing tag. In such cases, we can use a XML validator.

7. JavaScript Object Notation (JSON)

As the name suggests, JSON is an object notation (or symbol) for JavaScript. JSON was mainly developed for JavaScript. It helps JavaScript to communicate with server. We will now discuss how a JSON file is made and how it is implemented in our JavaScript code.

JSON Syntax

A JSON can be defined as an individual file with json [.json] extension or, within JavaScript an object can be defined and JSON can be assigned to it. Both of these JSONs will have the same structure. Let us understand JSON with an example:

From above example, we can derive following:

- JSON Data is in name value pair (e.g. "name": "Batman")
- JSON Data are separated via commas
- Curly braces hold JSON objects
- Square brackets hold JSON arrays
- JSON values can be one of the following:

o a string (written within double or single quotes [e.g. "Batman" or 'Batman', both are correct])

o a number (written without any quote e.g. "age": 53)

o an object (JSON object e.g. "Emp_detail" here is an object)

Note: We can even have an array of object or object of arrays. If an object has multiple arrays, it will be called object of arrays. And if, an array includes multiple objects, it will be called an array of objects. We will learn more about this in upcoming assignment section.

o an array (JSON array e.g. "powers" here is an array)

Note: We can even have an array of array i.e. array inside an array. We will learn more about this in upcoming assignment section.

o a Boolean (It can have true or false as a value, e.g. "active")

o null (It can be also assigned, if values are not available; e.g. Middle name for a person can be a null)

In generic, JSON syntax can be defined as below:

Here, name can be any unique string, and value can be either a string, number, array or object.

JavaScript Object

In JavaScript, an object is an entity with its own properties and types. Let us take an example to understand this:

Here we have defined an object myBike with its four properties. These properties are too in the form of a key-value pair. We will discuss JavaScript objects in detail under JavaScript section, later.

Conversion between JSON and JavaScript Object

We can only exchange a text between a browser and a server, and JSON is a text-based format which represents structured data on JavaScript syntax. In JavaScript, data manipulation is done mainly with the help of JavaScript Object. Once, we are done with data manipulation, we convert our JavaScript object to JSON and send it to the server.

It is very important to convert JSON to JavaScript Object and vice versa. Following are the two important methods to perform these operations:

- JSON.parse(): JSON to JavaScript Object

It accepts JSON string as a parameter and returns corresponding JavaScript object.

- JSON.stringify(): JavaScript Object to JSON

It accepts a JavaScript object as a parameter and returns corresponding JSON string data.

Important Points to Remember:

- To access JSON data that is parsed as a JS object into a variable in JavaScript, we use dot/bracket notation as shown below.
- To drill down further, we need to chain the required property name with the required index of the array together. This is explained below:

Note: All codes are written directly into the console of a browser so that, instantly an error can be identified.

- It is mandatory to use double quotes [single quotes are not valid] around strings and property names in JSON.
- Even a single comma can cause a JSON file to go wrong. Therefore, it is very important to use a JSON validator, before passing JSON to our code. A JSON validator like jsonlint.com, helps us to identify errors within our JSON code.

JSON Use

A JSON data can be used to load data into a table or wherever required. Below you can find the output for the JSON we have mentioned in the intro part of JSON:

JSON Assignment

Assignment 1: Develop a JSON Data which shows data of students from three different sections of a class. Data must include students name and their favourite subjects. Display the data in a table.

Solution: In this assignment, we will initially have a JSON with three objects (represented by {}). These objects will represent three different sections, so we will name these objects as A, B and C.

Under these objects, we will have an array. An array (represented by []) can hold multiple records. Thus, we will have multiple students record under each array.

Each individual record for a student is also unique, therefore every student information will also be represented using an object. Here, we have added only three students (objects) in each section.

If I add three students in place of three empty objects, it will look something like this:

Since, these objects represent students' detail, therefore I named them students. Under this object, we will have another array (here, fav sub) that will represent their favourite subjects.

If we add all the subjects in the given array, fav sub. Then, it will look something like this:

Now, we will validate the above JSON code using the validator. Our JSON will produce output something like this (not exactly, we have added section to make it look better):

Assignment 2: Develop a JSON Data which shows data of 10 Employees. It will include Employee ID, Employee Name, Date of Joining and their location. The output must look something like this (but with 10 record):

Note: You can use online JSON to HTML converter to check output in the form of a table.

***

Before moving to the next section, let us evaluate what we have learned till now:

- HTML: Using it, you have already designed a layout of Google Form
- CSS: Using it, you have added layout styles in above Form

- XML: We have not added any task for this, it is an important part of framework-based development
- JSON: Using it, you have created a data structure of Employee Details

Now, we will add some dynamic feature in our UI using a scripting language.

8. JavaScript (JS)

JavaScript is a scripting language (or dynamic programming language) which when applied to an HTML document, can make it interactive for users. Scripting or dynamic programming language are the one which can perform operations during runtime unlike a compile time programming language. ECMAScript is the official name of JavaScript.

Setup

To implement JavaScript in our HTML document, we need to call it the way we did for CSS. First, go to the folder where we have done project setup (If you forgot what I am talking about, check CSS section). Once you reach at the required folder location, follow the given steps to complete the setup:

1. Create a text file under folder scripts and name it index.js.
2. In your index.html file enter the given element, under <body > </body> tag.

```
<script src="scripts/index.js"></script>
```

Note: Write the above statement, just above </body> tag. It is done because, we will let the

HTML document to load first and then load the script data, this will load the UI faster.

Now, whatever you write in index.js will be reflected into index.html. We will mainly write our code in console of browser (press F12 in Chrome to open its console), this will help us to validate our code there itself.

Basic Operations using JavaScript

Let's explain some of the important JavaScript operations, this will give you a better understanding of how it all works. We will go through all the basic concepts of JavaScript first and then in assignment section we will implement them.

Display Output using JavaScript

To display anything on our screen, we were earlier using HTML or XML and even CSS. Now, we can also use JavaScript to display output in our website. JavaScript helps us to display dynamic output i.e. output is not static and can be changed according to the requirement at runtime. For example, we can take two numbers as input and display their sum using JavaScript.

Following are the different JavaScript based output possibilities:

• Writing into an HTML element [using innerHTML]

In HTML & CSS section, we have discussed how to access an HTML element using its id. Now, we will use the same id to display our output within that element. Syntax is shown below:

document.getElementByld("<your_element_nam e>").innerHTML

You will better understand this concept from given example. For given HTML code, the output is shown just below to it:

Output:

Now, there is a requirement to change "The God of Cricket" to "The Lord of Cricket". In this case, we will access this element via its id that is "idH2" (as per the code shown above). Let us directly code in the browser console and check the output there itself.

In the first line, we have checked what is the value of HTML for element "idH2". In the second line, we have replaced the earlier value with our required value. The new output is shown below:

- Writing into the HTML output [using document.write()]

This statement is used mainly for test purpose as it removes all the existing HTML with the given value. The syntax is given below:

document.write("<your_text>"):

We have used above syntax to print a static statement below:

- Writing into an alert box [using window.alert()]

Many times, there is a requirement to print a message as an information for a user to alert him. This is where alert box comes into the picture. The syntax is as shown below:

```
windows.alert("<your_alert_text");
```

- Writing into the browser console [using console.log()]

This is the most preferred way to check the output while debugging your JavaScript code. We will show its use while discussing the debugger section.

```
Console.log("<your_output_text");
```

Accessing HTML tag in JavaScript

To dynamically change the content of our webpage, we will have to access an HTML tag. It can be easily achieved by finding an HTML tag with its element ID. Thus, we will also have to assign an ID to the HTML tag for which we want to change the content using JavaScript. This will be clearer from the example mentioned below:

```
document.getElementById("idH2").innerHTML =
"Hello India";
```

In the above example, we search for an element by its ID in the whole HTML document and then replace its inner HTML content with the text in the right side of equal to sign (=), here "Hello India".

Performing Basic Window function

The Window object is supported by all the browsers and is used to represent a browser's window. We can perform various functions using the Window Objects. Following are the widely used Window functions with their description:

Window Function Description Example

window.alert( ) This method displays an alert box with your message and OK button. window.alert("Hello World");

window.confirm( ) This method displays a dialog box with an optional message and two buttons i.e. OK and Cancel. if (window.confirm("Do you want to exit?")) {window.alert("Thanks for Visiting!"); }

window.prompt( ) This method opens a dialog box that prompts a user for input. prompt("What's your name?");

window.print( ) This method prints the current screen. window.print( );

window.open( ) This method is used to open a new browser window or a new tab. This is mainly used to open a link in a new tab. window.open("https://gocoding.org");

window.close( ) This method closes the current window. This only works if the window was opened using window.open(). newWindow = window.open("", "newWindow", "width=200, height=100");
newWindow.close();

window.history.back( ) This method loads the previous URL from the history list.
window.history.back();
window.history.forward( ) This method loads the next URL from the history list.
window.history.forward();
window.localStorage( ) This method is used to store & retrieve data (key/ value pair) from the browser's local storage.
window.localStorage.setItem('myName', 'Rudra');
window.localStorage.getItem('myName');
window.sessionStorage( ) This is same as the above function, the difference is that the data gets deleted once the session is closed (i.e. browser's tab is closed)
window.sessionStorage.setItem('myName' , 'Rudra');
window.sessionStorage.getItem('myName');
*Note: Please try the above examples in your browser's console.

Defining variables in JavaScript

A variable in JavaScript is an empty container that can be used to store anything. It can store a number, character(string), Boolean, array or object.

A variable in JavaScript can be declared using var keyword.

var myName = "Rudra";

In the example above, we have created a variable "myName" and have an assigned it a value "Rudra" which is a string. Unlike other programming languages, we don't have to specify data type for variables in JavaScript. It automatically takes the data type according to the value. Following are the data types supported by JavaScript variables:

Data Type Description Example

Undefined When a variable has not been assigned any value, then it has the value undefined. Undefined is set by JavaScript. var myName;

Here myName has the value undefined.

Null It represents intentional absence of any object value. Unlike undefined, it is assigned to a variable and not set by JavaScript. var tax = null;

Number A numeric digit that is represented without any quote around them. var myMarks = 90;

String It is a collection of characters. It is represented with quote marks. var

Boolean It is true/false value and is written without quotes. It is often used as a flag: to represent if an action is done or not. var myHoliday = true;

Array It is a structure that allows to store multiple values into a single variable. It is represented by

[ ]. It is a list and the position of its items lies between 0 to n. var mySubjects = [Maths, English, Science, JavaScript]

Object An object is a collection of properties. These properties can be added or removed. A JavaScript object is a mapping between keys and values separated by a colon. It can be created either using object literals i.e. { } or JavaScript keyword new. var employee = {name: “Rudra”, age: 25};

or

var employee = new Object();
employee.name = “Rudra”;
employee.age = 25;

Performing Maths Operation

In this section, we will explore all the mathematical operators and mathematical functions available in JavaScript.

Mathematical Operators in JavaScript

To perform mathematical operation, we will need all the mathematics operators, that we know. It can be divided into given five sections:

1. JavaScript Arithmetic Operators

These operators are used to perform Arithmetic operations of numbers.

Operator	Description	Example
+	Addition	4 + 2 = 6
-	Subtraction	4 - 2 = 2
*	Multiplication	4 * 2 = 8

/ Division 4 / 2 = 2
% Modulus (Division Remainder) 4 % 2
= 0
++ Increment 4++ = 5
-- Decrement 4-- = 3

2. JavaScript Assignment Operators

These operators are used to assign values to a variable in JavaScript.

Operator Description Example
= a = b a = 3
+= a += b □ a = a + b a += 3 □ a = a + 3
-= a -= b □ a = a- b a -= 3 □ a = a 3
*= a *= b □ a = a* b a *= 3 □ a = a * 3
/= a /= b □ a = a / b a /= 3 □ a = a / 3
%= a%=b □a = a %b a %= 3 □ a = a %3

3. JavaScript Comparison Operators

These operators are used to perform basic comparisons between any two numbers. In given examples, we assume that value of X = 4.

Operator Description Example
Result
== Equal to X == 5
X == 4
X == "4" False
True
True
=== Equal value and equal type X === 4
X === "4" Ture
False

!= Not equal X != 5 True

!== Not equal value or not equal type X !==
4
X !== "4"
X !== 5 False
True
True

\> Greater than X > 5 False

< Less than X < 5 True

\>= Greater than or Equal to X >= 5 False

<= Less than or Equal to X <= 5 True

? Ternary Operator

Syntax:
condition ? exprT : exprF
? stands for If True than
: stands for If False than var age = 25;
var beverage = (age >= 21) ? "Beer" : "Juice";
console.log(beverage); Beer

4. JavaScript Logical Operators

Logical operators are used to determine the logic between two variables, values or conditions. In some cases, we need to add two or more comparisons for same variables and in that case, we use JavaScript logical operators.

In given examples we have assumed the value of x = 2 and y = 4.

Operator	Description	Example	Result
&&	and	(x < 5 && y > 1)	True
||	or	(x == 4 || y == 2)	False

! not !(x == y) True

5. JavaScript Bitwise Operators

The bitwise operators are very similar to the JavaScript Logical operators, except they work on a smaller scale i.e. binary representation of data.

Following are the operators with their functionality:

Operator Functionality

op1 & op2 It compares two bits and generates a result of 1 if both bits are 1, else it returns 0.

op1 | op2 It compares two bits and generates a result of 1 if bits are complementary, else 0.

op1^ op2 It compares two bits and generates a result of 1 if only either of the bits are 1, else 0.

~op1 It inverts all the bits of the operand (the number).

op1 >> op2 It moves the bits to the right, discards the far-right bit, and assigns the leftmost bit a value of 0.

op1 << op2 It moves the bits to the left, discards the far-left bit, and assigns the rightmost bit a value of 0.

Note: Both operands associated with the bitwise operator must be integers. All the bits, of an integer, are compared individually.

Operator Description Example Bitwise Representation Result Decimal

& AND 5 & 1 0101 & 0001 0001 1

| OR 5 | 1 0101 | 0001 0101 5
~ NOT ~ 5 ~0101 1010 10
^ XOR 5 ^ 1 0101 ^ 0001 0100 4
<< Zero fill left shift 5 << 1 0101 << 1 1010 10
>> Signed right shift 5 >> 1 0101 >> 1 0010 2
>>> Zero fill right shift 5 >>> 1 0101 >>> 1 0010 2

JavaScript String Operation

A JavaScript String is zero or more characters written within quotes. We can perform following operations on string:

Operation Description Example

String Length We can get length of any string stored in a variable.

Syntax: var.length

Here, var can be any variable. var txt = "Gargi";

var sln = txt.length;

Output: 5

Finding a String in a String We can get index (position) of a text in a string.

Syntax:

indexOf(): Returns first occurrence of the text

lastIndexOf():Returns last occurrence of the text var str = "You will locate me!";

var pos = str.indexOf("locate");

Output: 9

Slice (start, end) It extracts a part of a string and returns the extracted part in a new string. It takes two parameters: the starting position and the end position [excluding the end position value] var str = "I am Rudra!";
var res = str.slice(5, 10);
Output: Rudra
Substring (start, end) It is similar to slice(), but it cannot accept negative indexes unlike slice operation. var str = "I am Rudra!";
var res = str. substring (5, 10);
Output: Rudra
Substr (start, length) It is similar to slice(). Here, the second parameter is the length of the text to be extracted. var str = "I am Rudra!";
var res = str. substr(5, 10);
Output: Rudra!
Replace () It replaces a specified value with another value in a string.
It is case sensitive and replaces only the first finding. It doesn't change the original but returns the change into a new variable. var str = "I am German";
var n = str.replace("German", "Indian");
Output: I am Indian
Converting Case To convert a case, we can use the following:
1. toUpperCase()
2. toLowerCase() var text = "Hello World!";
var uText = text.toUpperCase();
var ltext = text.toLowerCase();

Concat () It joins two or more strings together. var text1 = "Hello";
var text2 = "India";
var text3 = text1.concat(" ", text2);
Trim () It removes whitespaces from both side of a given string. var str = " Hello India ";
alert(str.trim());
Split () It splits a string based on a condition mentioned within the brackets. var txt = "a,b,c,d,e";
txt.split(","); // Split on commas
txt.split(" "); // Split on spaces
txt.split("|");// Split on pipe
txt.split("");// Split in characters

JavaScript Numeric Operation

We have already performed several arithmetic operations on numbers till now. Apart from this, JavaScript provides following operations on numbers:

Operation Description Example
toString() It returns numbers as strings. var x = 123;
var y = x.toString();
Output: “123”
toFixed() It rounds a number to a given number of digits and returns it in the form of a string. var x = 9.656;
x.toFixed(0); Output: 10
x.toFixed(2); Output: 9.66

valueOf()   It returns the value of a variable
var x = 123;
x.valueOf();
Output: 123
Number()   It converts variables into a number. It can also convert a date into a number.
Number(new Date("2019-05-01"));
Output: 1556668800000
parseInt()   It parses a string and returns a whole number. It returns only the first number.
parseInt("10.33");
Output: 10

JavaScript Regular Expression (RegEx)

A regular expression is a collection of characters that forms a search pattern. This search pattern can be used to perform text search, text replace and text validation operations, as shown below:

Operation   Description   Example
search()   We can do a case sensitive search by using an identifier i. In this case we don't have to search the exact data.   var str = "Search Me!";
var n = str.search("/me/i");
Output: 7
replace()   We can replace a string using a case insensitive expression.   var str = "Replace Me!";
var res = str.replace(/me/i, "Yourself");
Output: Replace Yourself!

test() We can test if a given string has a presence of required character or not. var email = "myemail@gmail.com";
var res = (/@/.test(email));
Output: true

JavaScript Operation on Array

A JavaScript Array is used to store multiple values in a single variable.

Example: Array of single digit numbers

myArray = [0, 1, 2, 3, 4, 5, 6, 7, 8, 9]

Creating an Array

An array can be created using following two ways:

1. Using array literal

var myArray = [ ];

2. Using JavaScript Keyword new

var myArray = new Array( );

Access an element of an Array

An element of an array can be accessed by referring its position also known as index number. Suppose, we have an array myArray of different computer languages.

myArray = [“C”, “C++”, “JavaScript”, “ABAP”, “Java”];

The index of an array starts from 0. Therefore, [0] will be the first element and [1] will be the second element.

We can access any of the element by referring its index as shown below:

myElement = myArray[2];

Output: “JavaScript”

Looping Array Elements

To Loop each of the element, we can use a for loop as shown below:

Example: In given example we will check if the array of devices has laptop or not.

```
var device = ["mobile", "computer", "laptop",
"earphone"]
var dLength = device.length;
for (i = 0; i < dLength; i++)
{
If (device[i] = "laptop")
console.log("Yes, array has laptop as a device!");
}
```

Operations on JavaScript Array

We can perform following operations on an Array:

In given examples, we will perform operations on an array numbers = [1,2,3,4];

Operation Description Example

pop() This method removes the last element of an array. numbers.pop();

Output: [1,2,3]

push() This method adds a new element in the end. numbers.push(5);

Output: [1,2,3,4,5]

length This is a property of array and it returns the length of an array. numbers.length;

Output: 4

shift() This method removes the first element of an array and shifts all the other elements to the lower index. numbers.shift();

Output: [2,3,4]

unshift() This method adds a new element at the beginning. numbers.unshift(0);

Output: [0,1,2,3,4]

forEach() This method calls a function once for each array element.

```
numbers.forEach(function(num){
if(num == 2)
console.log("2 is there");
});
```

Output: 2 is there

toString() This method converts an array to a string of array values separated by comma. number.toString();

Output: 1,2,3,4

delete This method converts an element to undefined. It is recommended to pop() or shift() to remove an element in place of delete.

```
delete numbers[0];
console.log(numbers[0]);
```

Output: undefined

splice(a,b) This method is used to delete and insert new items.

Here a is the index where we want to insert/delete items and b is the number of elements that will be deleted.

Anything added after these parameters i.e. a and b will be inserted at the index a. 1. Deleting items

numbers.splice(0,1);
console.log(numbers);
Output: [2,3,4]

2. Adding items

numbers.splice(0,1,-1);
console.log(numbers);
Output: [-1,2,3,4]

slice(a,b) This method slices out a part of an array into a new array. Here, a is the index from where the slice begins and b is the index where it ends, excluding b. If there is no ending index i.e. b, then all the rest elements beginning from a is sliced. var newSet = numbers.slice(1,3)
console.log(newSet);
Output: [2,3]

concat() This method concatenates two arrays into a new array. var numbers2 = [5,6,7,8]
var mergeSet = numbers.concat(numbers2);
console.log(mergeSet);
Output: [1, 2, 3, 4, 5,6,7,8]

sort() This method sorts an array alphabetically/numerically in ascending order. var set = [1,2,3,4,0];
set.sort();
console.log(set);
Output: [0,1,2,3,4]

reverse() This method reverses the elements of an array.
This method can be used to sort an array in descending order which is already sorted in ascending order. numbers.reverse();
console.log(numbers);
Output: [4,3,2,1]
indexOf() This method searches for an element value and returns its position into a new variable. var a = numbers.indexOf(1);
console.log(a);
Output: 0

JavaScript Operation on Date
In JavaScript we can fetch current date and time based on the browser's time zone. This date is displayed as a full text string.
Example: Fri May 03 2019 22:22:06 GMT+0530 (India Standard Time)
We can create a new Date object in given four ways:
Date Object Description Example
new Date() This method returns current date and time based on the browser's time zone. console.log(new Date());
Output: The current date and time will be displayed
new Date(year, month, day, hours, minutes, seconds, milliseconds) This method creates a new Date object with a specified date and time.

var date = new Date(2019, 06, 07, 10, 33, 30, 0);
console.log(data);
Output: Sun Jul 07 2019 10:33:30 GMT+0530 (India Standard Time)

new Date(milliseconds) This method adds/subtracts milliseconds mentioned here from the current date. console.log(new Date(1000));
Output: The current date and time + 1000 milliseconds will be dispalyed

new Date(date string) This method creates a new date from a date string. This date string should be of given formats only:

1. ISO Date: "2019-04-30"
2. Short Date: "04/30/2019"
3. Long Date: "Apr 30 2019" or "25 Apr 2015"

console.log(new Date("Apr 30 2019"));
Output: Tue Apr 30 2019 00:00:00 GMT+0530 (India Standard Time)

Chapter 4: Javascript Functions

In JavaScript, you write all your logic within a function. A function is a block of code designed to perform a specific task. After performing its task, the function returns a result. To execute a function, we need to trigger it. In this section, we will learn how to write a function, how to trigger a function and how to get a result from that function.

JavaScript Function Syntax

A JavaScript function starts with a keyword function, it is followed by the function name and parentheses ( ). The code that needs to be executed is written within curly brackets { }.

```
function add(a, b){
return a + b;
}
```

This function has two parameters a and b, known as arguments of a function. The values of these parameters will be provided while calling this function. In return, this function will produce sum of these parameters.

Triggering a JavaScript Function

A JavaScript function is triggered in the following three ways:

1. When an event occurs i.e. when a user clicks a button
2. The function is called by another JavaScript function

3. Automatically (self-invoked) [In case, function is triggered by JavaScript events]

JavaScript Function Return

The JavaScript return statement is used to return the result of a function. This is mainly used whenever the function is called from another function or variable.

JavaScript Objects

A JavaScript object is a variable which stores multiple data in the form of key and value pairs separated by a colon.

This key (or name) value pair together is called property of an object.

Example: An object with Employee Data

var person = {firstName: "Priyanka", lastName: "Pandey", age: 22, education:"MCA"};

Creating an Object

We can create an object using given three ways:

1. Using Object Initializers

In this method of object creation, we directly create a variable and define it like an object with key and value pair.

var obj = {key1: "value1", key2: "value2", ……, keyN: "valueN"};

var person = {firstName: "Hitesh", lastName: "Goel", age: 23}

or, simply by defining a variable and assigning it an empty object as shown below:

var obj = {};

2. Using a constructor function

In this method of object creation, we follow given two steps:

a. We define the object type by writing a constructor function.

b. Create an instance of the object with new.

Example: An object person with its properties

Constructor Function

```
function employee(firstName, lastName, dob) {
 this.firstName = firstName;
 this.lastName = lastName;
 this.dob = dob;
}
```

Instance of the Constructor

```
var person = new employee('Aditya', 'Farrad', 1994);
```

In the above example, we have created a JavaScript function and named it employee. Then for every new object creation, we will call this function with the values. Here the keys are fixed as firstName, lastName and dob. this in the function is a JavaScript keyword which refers to the current object.

3. Using the object.create method

This method creates a new object using an existing object as a prototype.

var newPerson = Object.create(person);

Here, we have created a new object newPerson using the object person created in the method 1 above as a prototype.

Access an element of an Object

We can access an element [in case of object, property] of an object in given two ways:

A. objectName.propertyName

Example: person.firstName;

B. objectName["propertyName"]

Example: person[“firstName”];

JavaScript Events

In our browser, anything we do is with the HTML. This HTML part has some predefined events to handle user interactions. Following are some of the HTML events:

Event	Description
onchange	This event is triggered when an HTML element has been changed
onclick	This event is triggered when a user clicks an HTML element
onmouseover	This event is triggered when the user moves the mouse over an HTML element
onmouseout	This event is triggered when the user moves the mouse away from an HTML element
onkeydown	This event is triggered when the user pushes a keyboard key
onload	This event is triggered when the browser has finished loading the page

A JavaScript function can be assigned to handle these events. For that to happen, we need to do the following:

1. Load our JavaScript in the HTML body section [We have done this part in JavaScript setup earlier].
2. Add the event attribute to your HTML and assign it the JavaScript function that you want to call.

Syntax:

```
<element event='JavaScript function'>
```

3. Write a function with the same name assigned to the HTML event attribute and your required code within the function.

To understand the HTML events better, we will create a simple program.

Example: Create a Program to take two inputs and print their sum on click of a button.

HTML Code:

```
<!DOCTYPE html>
<html>
<head>
<link href="styles/style.css" rel="stylesheet"
type="text/css">
<script src="scripts/index.js"></script>
</head>
<body>
<div>
<h1 id="idH1"> Addition Program</h1>
<h2 id="idH2"> Enter Two Numbers and Click the
Sum button </h2>
```

```
<label>Enter First Number</label>
<Input id="idinput1"/>
<BR/>
<BR/>
<label>Enter Second Number</label>
<Input id="idinput2"/>
<BR/>
<BR/>
<button onclick="onSum()">Sum</button>
<BR/>
<BR/>
<label>Result :</label>
<label id="idResult" ></label>
</div>
</body>
</html>
```

CSS Code:

```
h1 {
 color: red;
 padding-left: 10px;
}

h2 {
 color: blue;
 padding-left: 10px;
}
```

JavaScript Code:

```
function onSum(){
```

```
var num1 =
Number(document.getElementById("idinput1").v
alue);
var num2 =
Number(document.getElementById("idinput2").v
alue);
document.getElementById("idResult").innerHTML
= num1+num2;
}
```

Output Screen before clicking the button:

Output Screen after clicking the button:

JavaScript Assignments

In this section, we will continue building our very first assignment. This time, we will write the full code for HTML, CSS and JavaScript altogether.

Assignment 1: Create a Sign-up form, with following validation:

- All fields are mandatory
- The Email Id must be valid
- The Phone number must be valid
- The Date of Birth must be in such a way that it is greater than 18
- The two passwords must match (password and confirm password)

HTML Code:

```
<!DOCTYPE html>
<html>
<head>
```

```
<link href="styles/style.css" rel="stylesheet"
type="text/css">
<script src="scripts/index.js"></script>
</head>
<body>
<form style="border:1px solid #000">
 <div class="container">
   <h1>Sign Up</h1>
   <p>All fields are mandatory! </p>
   <hr>
<div>
<div class="top-row">
   <div class="field-wrap">
<input type="text" placeholder="First Name"
required>
   <input type="text" placeholder="Last Name"
required>
   </div>
   </div>
<div class="top-row">
   <div class="field-wrap">
   <input type="email" placeholder="Enter Email
ID" required autocomplete="off">
<input id="idNumber" type="number"
placeholder="Enter Phone Number" required>
   </div>
   </div>
<div class="top-row">
   <div class="field-wrap">
```

```
<input id="psd1" type="password" placeholder="Enter Password" name="psw" required>
  <input id="psd2" type="password" placeholder="Confirm Password" name="psw-repeat" required>
  </div>
  </div>
<div class="top-row">
  <div class="field-wrap">
 <label for="start">Enter your Date of Birth: </label>
<input type="date" id="start" name="trip-start"
   value="2018-07-22"
    min="1900-01-01" max="2001-12-31">
  </div>
  </div>
<div class="clearfix">
  <button type="button" class="cancelbtn">Cancel</button>
  <button type="submit" class="signupbtn" onclick="onSignup()">Sign Up</button>
  </div>
 </div>
</form>
<!-- The Modal -->
<div id="myModal" class="modal">
 <!-- Modal content -->
 <div class="modal-content">
  <span class="close">&times;</span>
  <p>You are Registered successfully!</p>
```

```
  </div>
</div>
</body>
</html>
```

CSS Code:

```
.field-wrap {
  position:relative;
  margin-bottom:40px;
}

.top-row {
  &:after {
    content: "";
    display: table;
    clear: both;
  }

  > div {
    float:left;
    width:48%;
    margin-right:4%;
    &:last-child {
      margin:0;
    }
  }
}
h1,p{
text-align: center;
}
body {font-family: Arial, Helvetica, sans-serif;}
```

```
* {box-sizing: border-box}

/* Full-width input fields */
input[type=text], [type=email], [type=number],
[type=date], input[type=password] {
  width: 500px;
  padding: 15px;
  margin: 5px 0 22px 0;
  border: none;
  background: #f1f1f1;
}

input[type=text]:focus, [type=email]:focus,
[type=number]:focus, [type=date]:focus,
input[type=password]:focus {
  background-color: #ddd;
  outline: none;
}

hr {
  border: 1px solid #f1f1f1;
  margin-bottom: 25px;
}

/* Set a style for all buttons */
button {
  background-color: #4CAF50;
  color: white;
  padding: 14px 20px;
  margin: 8px 0;
  border: none;
```

```
  cursor: pointer;
  width: 100%;
  opacity: 0.9;
}

button:hover {
  opacity:1;
}

/* Extra styles for the cancel button */
.cancelbtn {
  padding: 14px 20px;
  background-color: #f44336;
}

/* Float cancel and signup buttons and add an
equal width */
.cancelbtn, .signupbtn {
  float: left;
  width: 50%;
}

/* Add padding to container elements */
.container {
  padding: 16px;
}

/* Clear floats */
.clearfix::after {
  content: "";
  clear: both;
```

```
 display: table;
}

/* Change styles for cancel button and signup button on extra small screens */
@media screen and (max-width: 300px) {
 .cancelbtn, .signupbtn {
   width: 100%;
 }
}
/* The Modal (background) */
.modal {
 display: none; /* Hidden by default */
 position: fixed; /* Stay in place */
 z-index: 1; /* Sit on top */
 padding-top: 100px; /* Location of the box */
 left: 0;
 top: 0;
 width: 100%; /* Full width */
 height: 100%; /* Full height */
 overflow: auto; /* Enable scroll if needed */
 background-color: rgb(0,0,0); /* Fallback color */
 background-color: rgba(0,0,0,0.4); /* Black w/ opacity */
}

/* Modal Content */
.modal-content {
 background-color: #fefefe;
 margin: auto;
 padding: 20px;
```

```
  border: 1px solid #888;
  width: 80%;
}

/* The Close Button */
.close {
  color: #aaaaaa;
  float: right;
  font-size: 28px;
  font-weight: bold;
}

.close:hover,
.close:focus {
  color: #000;
  text-decoration: none;
  cursor: pointer;
}
```

JavaScript Code:

```
function onSignup(){
var number, pwd1, pwd2;
number                                                     =
document.getElementById("idNumber");
pwd1 = document.getElementById("psd1");
pwd2 = document.getElementById("psd2");
if(number.value.length !== 10)
alert("Wrong Mobile Number!");
else
{if (pwd1 !== pwd2)
alert("Password Do not match!");
```

```
else
{
// Get the modal
var modal =
document.getElementById('myModal');
// Get the button that opens the modal
var btn = document.getElementById("myBtn");
// When the user clicks the button, open the
modal
 modal.style.display = "block";
 }
}
}
```

Output without any input

Output with validation Error Message

1. When Sign up is clicked without any input data

2. When Sign up is clicked with wrong Email ID

3. When Sign up is clicked with wrong Date of Birth

Output with Success Message

When all the input fields are validated, then a dummy message is shown saying “You are Registered successfully”

Assignment 2: Create a calculator, with the following validation:

- On click of c i.e. clear, the input box must get empty
- On division of any number by 0 must produce error message
- If result is too big or small to show, produce valid message

The calculator must look something like shown below:

What to do next?

If you have reached to this milestone, then you are now a competent Website developer. I will suggest to explore more about website development and learn about other web development technologies such as node.js, react.js, php, etc. This will help to open your logical thinking in terms of website functionalities. I will also suggest to go through multiple websites and try to replicate using what you have learned. The website world is very colourful, it is time to experience them all. Happy learning!

Chapter 5: What Is Html?

What is Hyper Text?

Hyper Text means a special text which has:

Link to other resources in the Internet.

It can include Videos, Images and Sounds.

The most important part of HyperText is the ability to link other resources on the server which can be accessed via the link.

Hypertext are displayed on the computer screen mostly Browser like Chrome from Google, Edge from Microsoft and Firefox.

Learn more about the Hypertext from here.

How Web Works?

The main purpose of Web or World Wide Web (WWW) is to exchange information from one computer to another computer.

WWW is the way of connecting all the documents and displaying them on the browser.

Web uses HTTP protocol to transfer the information over the Internet.

Hypertext are transferred from one computer to another via the HTTP protocol and displayed on the browser. This how Web Works:

You Type the Website name in the Browser. Eg. www.wpfreelancer.com

Browser sends the request to DNS Server.

DNS Server search for IP address for this Domain Name.

Once the IP Address is found it then connects to the specific server in the Internet.

Server receives the request via the HTTP protocol.

Server will then search for the requested HyperText and send it back to the browser.

Browser will receive the hypertext and display it on the computer screen.

What is the purpose of Markup Language?

HyperText are typically exchanged between the servers to enable the communication between the machines.

But to make this HyperText convert into a language so that we can write the language in such a manner that we can get a specific task done.

Markup Language is used to represent how to organize the data. This kind of language focus more on how the data should be used and define the purpose of the data.

In Order to organize the HyperText that is sitting all over the computer into human understandable format a Markup Language was required.

HTML solves this problem of Marking up the required data from the server in such a manner that we understand the purpose of it.

For Example, We have a video file saved on the server. Now we want to tell everyone what is the purpose of this video and also some description of the Video when someone access this content.

Packing this information into a sample markup language could be like this

<title>How to Lose Weight in 10 Days</title>
<description>Quick and Easy way to lose weight without going to gym</description>
<videolocation>/assets/video/looseweight.mpeg</videolocation>

This is a Markup Language but not HTML. We can pack our content in a Markup Language so that we understand the HyperText that we get from the server.

Learn more about Markup from here.

What is HTML?

HTML stands for Hyper Text Markup Language.

HTML is a Markup Language that is used to mark the contents and then tell the browser how to display them on the screen.

HTML is a markup language that our browser understands and know how to display them.

In HTML language, you will do the following things: Write how to display the contents on the browser.

Links to another resource on the server. (HyperLinks)

Embed Videos and Audio from the Server.

Layout the Content.

The main Purpose of HTML markup language is to tell browser how the data is displayed and in which location.

History of HTML?

English scientist Tim Berners-Lee invented the World Wide Web in 1989. He built a browser using which the resource where accessed over the internet and displayed on the browser.

In 1991, it was released to General Public.

From then, all the big companies released their own browsers like Google has Chrome and Windows released Edge.

Berners Lee released the first HTML sample page with 18 tags in it and displayed it on his own browser.

He defined HTML as

HTML is a markup language that web browsers use to interpret and compose text, images, and other material into visual or audible web pages

HTML5 is the latest version of HTML.

What is Web Server?

Web server is an application that is installed in the server which helps to listen to the HTTP request and send the HTTP response. It is meant to handle the web requests and pass over the hypertext by restricting and tracking the transactions.

Web server helps to track all the requests and additional details like IP address, location, browser details and many other details.

It also helps to manage the load, execute the code at server, and restrict the access before accessing the content at the server.

What is Web Application?

Application that is developed and deployed on Web Server are called as Web Applications.

Web Applications are small projects with bunch of files and media which are accessed via the Web Server.

What is Web Pages?

Web pages are the documents that can be displayed in the browser like Google Chrome, Edge or Safari.

Web pages are written using the HTML markup language and it is stored in the Web Server.

Then, Web pages are accessed in the Internet via a browser to display the output on the computer screen.

What is Web Site?

Web site is collection of Web pages. Each website is accessed with a Domain Name.

A logical grouping of web page to perform a desired functionality is called as website.

2.2 – Tag, Element and Attribute

What is Markup Language?

Markup language are written using the Markups. We mention marks before and after the content to show it has a special meaning to it.

Example of Markup:

<NAME>WPFREELANCER</NAME>

<SITE>WPFREELANCER.COM</SITE>

HTML is a Markup Language means everything you write using HTML will be with markups and write the content between the markups.

What is Tag?

A Tag is the text between the left angle bracket (<) and the right angle bracket (>). There are starting tags (such as <name>) and there are ending tags (</name>) Example:

<name>wpfreelancer.com</name>

<name> = Opening Tag

</name> = Closing Tag

What is Element?

An Element is the opening tag, the closing tag and anything in between.

What is Empty Element?

Element that does not have any data between the tags is called as Empty Element. <TAG /> is also called as self-closing element.

What is Attribute? An Attribute is a name=value pair inside the Element. Attribute help to show additional details about the element.

Example:

<dog>German Shepard</dog> = ELEMENT

<dog color="brown">German Shepard</dog> = ELEMENT with ATTRIBUTE

Color = "brown" is called as Attribute.

Summary:

2.3 – HTML Basic Structure

Purpose of HTML?

HTML was written to organize the data in such way that it can be properly displayed on the browser.

Using Markups in HTML, Elements can be arranged in such a manner that it can be logically shown how the final output looks like on computer screen.

Elements, tags, attributes of HTML were supposed to indicate how the title of the page looks like, how the heading should look and in which order.

Structure of Data?

HTML markup language uses a markup structure to organize the elements in the page.

Consider this example:

```
<html>
<head>
<title>Hello World!</title>
</head>
<body>
<h1>This is a heading</h1>
<p>This is a paragraph</p>
</body>
</html>
```

Do not worry about the HTML but focus more on how the elements are organized to tell browser about the purpose of each element and structure of each element.

The main purpose is to tell browser how to display the content on the computer screen so you organize the markups in the same way it should be displayed. Sequencing is also important which decide how the elements are organized on the page.

There is also a parent child relation between the elements.

head and body Elements are child for HTML p and h1 are child elements of body parent element.

2.4 – Setting up the System for Writing HTML

Install HTML Editor

To write the HTML pages you will need a HTML Editor. Follow this Steps to install the recommended HTML Editor.

Step 1: Visit http://brackets.io/

Go to http://brackets.io/

Step 2: Download the Brackets Software

Download the Brackets Software

Step 3: Install the Software

Once the installation file is downloaded, install the software on your desired location.

Click on Search and Type "Brackets". This will show the software that is installed.

Step 4: Open the Brackets Software

Step 5: Create the Folder and Open It

Once you open the Brackets software the first step is to point the editor to a folder on the system.

Create a folder in the system and Click on File -> Open Folder

Select the Folder where you want to store the files.

Verify the Folder Name from the Editor Title and Left side bar

Install Google Chrome Browser

Download and Install Google Chrome Browser https://www.google.com/chrome/

Alternative Editors

There are other Editors that you can also use to write HTML:

1. Visual Studio Code
2. Notepad++
3. Atom

Alternative Browsers

You need to test your html code all of these browser before releasing the code in production:

1. Firefox
2. Safari
3. Edge

Do I need Internet to run HTML programs?

• NO

You don't need Internet to Write and Run HTML Program on your local machine. You need Internet to download the software but not to write and run it.

2.5 – First HTML Page

Check the Software:

Make sure you have all the following software installed

1. Brackets HTML Editor 2. Google Chrome Browser

If you don't have these software then follow this guide to install it.

HTML Filename Convention:

HTML filename should be ".html" or ".htm" but always use ".html"

First HTML Page:

Step 1: Create the Folder and Open the Folder with Brackets

Option 1:

Create a Folder and Right Click on the Folder and Select “Open as Brackets Project”

Option 2:

Open the Brackets and go to File -> Open Folder

Step 2: Create an “index.html” file

Right Click and Select “New File”

Create the “index.html” file

Step 3: Copy the HTML code in the “index.html” file

DOWNLOAD THE SOURCE CODE

```
<!DOCTYPE html>
<html>
<head>
<title>Welcome to HTML!</title>
</head>
<body>
<h1>This is a Heading 1</h1>
<p>This is a Paragraph.</p>
</body>
</html>
```

LIVE PREVIEW

Sample Preview of the code in Brackets:

Step 4: Live Preview of the HTML Page

Click on the live preview button on the right hand side.

Try to change the text in the brackets editor and see how the changes are reflected live in the chrome browser.

Understanding of HTML Tags:

See how the instruction given in the HTML file has been displayed by the browser.

2.6 – HTML Parts

Sample HTML

We will review the parts of HTML. Here is the sample HTML.

```
<!DOCTYPE html>
<html>
<head>
<title>Welcome to HTML!</title>
</head>
<body>
<h1>This is a Heading 1</h1>
<p>This is a Paragraph.</p>
</body>
</html>
```

DOC TYPE

!DOCTYPE is the first declaration of the HTML page. This will indicate the browser what type of HTML version we are using.

If we want to tell browser to use different HTML version then we mention that in this DocType.

```
<!DOCTYPE html>
```

HTML

This is the root element and tell browser that this is a HTML document. All the HTML tags should be inside this element.

You should not define anything outside this element.

HEAD

Head element is used for the following things:

Include other supporting files required for this page.

Tell search engine about your page.

Set Title for your Page.

Mention the Meta data about your page.

All the elements you define in the HEAD tag are not displayed on the page.

BODY

This is the place where you define all the elements. Any element defined under body will be displayed on the page.

2.7 – HTML Boiler Plate

What is a Boiler Plate?

Boiler plate are like sample template that you can use as starting template to write your HTML page. Boiler plates save time because you don't have to type every time the same thing. It is a start point for writing the web page. You can always build your own boiler plate template but you can download some of the sample boiler plate from below.

Boiler Plate 1 – Empty Template

DOWNLOAD THE SOURCE CODE

```
<!DOCTYPE html>
<html>
<head>
```

```
</head>
<body>
</body>
</html>
```

LIVE PREVIEW

Boiler Plate 2 – Empty Template with Comments

DOWNLOAD THE SOURCE CODE

```
<!DOCTYPE html>
<html>
<head>
<!-- All Meta tags goes here -->
</head>
<body> <!-- All Content tags goes here -->
</body>
</html>
```

LIVE PREVIEW

Boiler Plate 3 – Empty Template with Title

DOWNLOAD THE SOURCE CODE

```
<!DOCTYPE html>
<html>
<head>
<!-- All Meta tags goes here -->
<title>My First Web Page</title>
</head>
<body>
<!-- All Content tags goes here -->
</body>
</html>
```

LIVE PREVIEW

Boiler Plate 4 – Empty Template with Meta Data

DOWNLOAD THE SOURCE CODE

```
<!DOCTYPE html> <html>
<head>
<!-- All Meta tags goes here -->
<meta charset="utf-8">
<meta name="viewport" content="width=device-width, initial-scale=1.0">
<meta name="description" content="First Web Page">
<title>My First Web Page</title>
</head>
<body>
<!-- All Content tags goes here -->
</body>
</html>
```

LIVE PREVIEW

Boiler Plate 5 – Page Template with Heading

DOWNLOAD THE SOURCE CODE

```
<!DOCTYPE html>
<html>
<head>
<!-- All Meta tags goes here --> <meta name="description" content="First Web Page">
<title>My First Web Page</title>
</head>
<body>
<!-- All Content tags goes here -->
<h1>Welcome to my First Page</h1>
</body>
</html>
```

LIVE PREVIEW:

Boiler Plate 6 – Page Template with Paragraph

DOWNLOAD THE SOURCE CODE

```
<!DOCTYPE html>
<html>
<head>
<!-- All Meta tags goes here -->
<meta charset="utf-8">
<meta name="viewport" content="width=device-
width, initial-scale=1.0">
<meta name="description" content="First Web
Page">
<title>My First Web Page</title> </head>
<body>
<!-- All Content tags goes here -->
<h1>Welcome to my First Page</h1>
<!-- https://www.lipsum.com/ -->
<p>Lorem Ipsum is simply dummy text of the
printing
and typesetting industry. Lorem Ipsum has been
the industry's standard dummy text ever since
the 1500s,
when an unknown printer took a galley of type
and
scrambled it to make a type specimen book.
</p>
</body>
</html>
```

LIVE PREVIEW:

Boiler Plate 7 – Standard HTML Template

DOWNLOAD THE SOURCE CODE

```
<!DOCTYPE html>
<html>
```

```
<head>        <meta        name="description"
content="Page Description">
<title>Page Title</title>
</head>
<body>
<h1>Heading</h1>
<p>Paragraph Text</p>
</body>
</html> LIVE PREVIEW
```

3. TEXT ELEMENTS

3 TEXT ELEMENTS

3.1 – HTML Text Elements

Purpose of HTML Text Elements

Purpose of HTML Text elements is to display text in a format that is appealing and readable.

There are different types of HTML Text Elements that help to display our content like we see the content in the newspaper and magazine.

Benefits of this Text Tags:

- Display Headings and Paragraphs
- Markup the Bold, Italics and Underlining the text.
- Show different format of text like Java code and normal readable text

Structural Markup

These are the markups that are used to define the text and give a real meaning to the text.

Like mentioning the Heading and Paragraphs on the Web Page.

Semantic Markup

Semantic elements are used to provide extra information to the user by bold text, underlines and italics. They increase the readability and also help to mark the text in the paragraphs or headings.

Like marking a Quotation can also be done via the Semantic Markup.

List of HTML Text Elements

These are the HTML Text Elements that you will learn in this section:

- Headings
- Horizontal Lines
- Paragraph
- Single Line Breaks
- Strong
- Emphasis
- Underline
- Italics
- Code
- Preformatted
- More Text Tags

One Page Text Elements:

This is just a sample to show how all the elements looks like in the Web Page. Next topics, you will learn all these elements one by one.

DOWNLOAD THE SOURCE CODE

```
<!DOCTYPE html>
```

```
<html>
<head> <meta charset="utf-8">
<meta name="viewport" content="width=device-width, initial-scale=1.0">
<meta name="description" content="Page Description">
<title>HTML Text Tags</title>
</head>
<body>
<!-- Headings -->
<h1>This is Heading 1.</h1>
<h2>This is Heading 2.</h2>
<h3>This is Heading 3.</h3>
<h4>This is Heading 4.</h4>
<h5>This is Heading 5.</h5>
<h6>This is Heading 6.</h6>
<!-- This is Horizontal Line -->
<h1>This is Horizontal Line.</h1>
<hr>
<!-- This is Paragraph -->
<h1>This is Paragraph.</h1>
<p>1. "Lorem ipsum dolor sit amet, consectetur adipisicing elit, sed do eiusmod tempor incididunt ut labore et dolore magna aliqua. Ut enim ad minim veniam, quis nostrud exercitation ullamco laboris nisi ut aliquip ex ea commodo consequat. Duis aute irure dolor in reprehenderit in voluptate velit esse cillum dolore eu fugiat nulla pariatur. Excepteur sint occaecat cupidatat non proident, sunt in culpa qui officia deserunt mollit anim id est laborum."</p>
```

```
<!-- This is Single Line Breaks -->
<h1>This is Single Line Breaks.</h1>
<br><br>
<!-- This is Strong -->
<h1>This is Strong.</h1>
<p>1. "<strong>Lorem</strong> ipsum dolor sit amet, consectetur adipisicing elit, sed do eiusmod tempor incididunt ut labore et dolore magna aliqua. Ut enim ad minim veniam, quis nostrud exercitation ullamco laboris nisi ut aliquip ex ea commodo consequat. Duis aute irure dolor in reprehenderit in voluptate velit esse cillum dolore eu fugiat nulla pariatur. Excepteur sint occaecat cupidatat non proident, sunt in culpa qui officia deserunt mollit anim id est laborum."</p>
<!-- This is Emphasis -->
<h1>This is Emphasis.</h1>
<p>I <strong>love</strong> to write <em>HTML5</em>!</p>
<!-- This is Underline -->
<h1>This is Undeline.</h1>
<p>I <u><strong>love</strong></u> to write <em>HTML5</em>!</p>
<!-- This is Italics --> <h1>This is Italics.</h1>
<p>I <i><u><strong>love</strong></u></i> to write <em>HTML5</em>!</p>
<!-- This is Code -->
<h1>This is Code.</h1>
<code>
public void add(int a, int b){
return a + b;
```

```
}
</code>
=
<!-- This is Pre -->
<h1>This is Preformatted.</h1>
<code>
<pre>
<!-- Check the Whitespace importance! -->
public void add(int a, int b)
{
return a + b;
}
int c = add(1, 2); </pre>
</code>
<h1>Some More Text Formatting Tags</h1>
<p><del>This text is deleted</del> and <ins>This
text is inserted</ins>.</p>
<p><s>This text has a strikethrough</s>.</p>
<p>Superscript<sup>®</sup>.</p>
<p>Subscript for things like
H<sub>2</sub>O.</p>
<p><small>This small text is small for for fine
print, etc.</small></p>
<p>Abbreviation: <abbr title="HyperText Markup
Language">HTML</abbr></p>
<p><q
cite="https://developer.mozilla.org/enUS/docs/H
TML/Element/q">This text is a short inline
quotation.</q></p>
<p><cite>This is a citation.</cite></p>
```

<p>The <dfn>dfn element</dfn> indicates a definition.</p>

<p>The <mark>mark element</mark> indicates a highlight.</p>

<p>The <var>variable element</var>, such as <var>x</var> = <var>y</var>.</p>

</body> </html>

This is Heading 1. This is Heading 2.

This is Heading 3.

This is Heading 4.

This is Heading 5.

This is Heading 6.

This is Horizontal Line.

This is Paragraph.

1. "Lorem ipsum dolor sit amet, consectetur adipisicing elit, sed do eiusmod tempor incididunt ut labore et dolore magna aliqua. Ut enim ad minim veniam, quis nostrud exercitation ullamco laboris nisi ut aliquip ex ea commodo consequat. Duis aute irure dolor in reprehenderit in voluptate velit esse cillum dolore eu fugiat nulla pariatur. Excepteur sint occaecat cupidatat non proident, sunt in culpa qui officia deserunt mollit anim id est laborum."

This is Single Line Breaks.

This is Strong.

1. "Lorem ipsum dolor sit amet, consectetur adipisicing elit, sed do eiusmod tempor incididunt ut labore et dolore magna aliqua. Ut enim ad minim veniam, quis nostrud exercitation ullamco laboris nisi ut aliquip ex ea commodo consequat.

Duis aute irure dolor in reprehenderit in voluptate velit esse cillum dolore eu fugiat nulla pariatur. Excepteur sint occaecat cupidatat non proident, sunt in culpa qui officia deserunt mollit anim id est laborum."

This is Emphasis.

I love to write HTML5!

This is Underline.

I love to write HTML5!

This is Italics.

I love to write HTML5!

This is Code.

```
public void add(int a, int b){
return a + b; }
```

This is Preformatted.

```
public void add(int a, int b)
{
return a + b;
}
int c = add(1, 2);
```

Some More Text Formatting Tags

This text is deleted and This text is inserted.

This text has a strikethrough.

Superscript®.

Subscript for things like H2O.

This small text is small for for fine print, etc.

Abbreviation: HTML

This text is a short inline quotation.

This is a citation.

The dfn element indicates a definition.

The mark element indicates a highlight.

The variable element, such as x = y. LIVE PREVIEW:

3.2 – Headings

Usage of Headings

Headings are used to display title of the paragraph or show some text in bigger size and bolder.

There are 6 headings tags <h1> to <h6>

h1 is the bigger and h6 being the smallest. Headings text tags are always big in size and use to grab attention of the user or show the purpose of the article.

The behavior of the headings can be change later using CSS which you will learn next.

Browser has a default settings to show headings.

Sample Example

DOWNLOAD THE EXAMPLE

```
<!DOCTYPE html>
<html>
<head>
<meta charset="utf-8">
<meta name="viewport" content="width=device-width, initial-scale=1.0">
<meta name="description" content="Page Description">
<title>Headings</title>
</head>
<body>
<!-- Observe the default style -->
```

```
<!-- Observe the font size -->
<!-- Observe the new lines -->
<h1>This is Heading 1.</h1>
<h2>This is Heading 2.</h2> <h4>This is Heading 4.</h4>
<h5>This is Heading 5.</h5>
<h6>This is Heading 6.</h6>
</body> </html>
```

3.3 – Horizontal Lines

Usage of Horizontal Line

Horizontal line acts like a separator between the sections and paragraph.

This is used when you want to add some space between the paragraphs and also show a line indicating a different topic.

TAG: <hr />

Remember that <hr> is a self-closing tag you don't need to close it.

Attributes of hr tag:

width = percent (%)

align = left, right, center

Sample Example

DOWNLOAD THE EXAMPLE

```
<!DOCTYPE html>
<html>
<head>
<meta charset="utf-8">
<meta name="viewport" content="width=device-width, initial-scale=1.0">
<meta name="description" content="Page Description">
```

```
<title>Horizontal Line</title>
</head>
<body>
<!-- Observe the spacing & line properties -->
<h1>This is Heading 1.</h1>
<hr>
<h2>This is Heading 2.</h2>
<hr>
<h3>This is Heading 3.</h3>
<hr>
<h4>This is Heading 4.</h4>
<hr>
<h5>This is Heading 5.</h5>
<hr> <hr width="50%" align="left">
</body>
</html> LIVE PREVIEW:
```

3.4 – Paragraphs

Usage of Paragraphs

Paragraphs is the place where you put most of your content to display on the browser.

Paragraph tags helps to organize the content nicely into small container which makes content easy to read and edit it.

TAG: <p>

ELEMENT: <p>sometext</p>

Sample Example

DOWNLOAD THE EXAMPLE

```
<!DOCTYPE html>
<html>
<head>
```

```
<meta charset="utf-8">
<meta name="viewport" content="width=device-
width, initial-scale=1.0"> <meta
name="description" content="Page Description">
<title>Paragraph</title>
</head>
<body>
<!-- Observe how the data is organized -->
<h1>Today's News</h1>
<p>1. It is a long established fact that a reader
will be distracted by the readable content of a
page when looking at its layout. The point of
using Lorem Ipsum is that it has a more-or-less
normal distribution of letters, as opposed to using
'Content here, content here', making it look like
readable English. Many desktop publishing
packages and web page editors now use Lorem
Ipsum as their default model text, and a search
for 'lorem ipsum' will uncover many web sites still
in their infancy. Various versions have evolved
over the years, sometimes by accident,
sometimes on purpose (injected humour and the
like).</p>
<p>2. It is a long established fact that a reader
will be distracted by the readable content of a
page when looking at its layout. The point of
using Lorem Ipsum is that it has a more-or-less
normal distribution of letters, as opposed to using
'Content here, content here', making it look like
readable English. Many desktop publishing
packages and web page editors now use Lorem
```

Ipsum as their default model text, and a search for 'lorem ipsum' will uncover many web sites still in their infancy. Various versions have evolved over the years, sometimes by accident, sometimes on purpose (injected humour and the like).</p>
<p>3. It is a long established fact that a reader will be distracted by the readable content of a page when looking at its layout. The point of using Lorem Ipsum is that it has a more-or-less normal distribution of letters, as opposed to using 'Content here, content here', making it look like readable English. Many desktop publishing packages and web page editors now use Lorem Ipsum as their default model text, and a search for 'lorem ipsum' will uncover many web sites still in their infancy. Various versions have evolved over the years, sometimes by accident, sometimes on purpose (injected humour and the like).</p>
</body>
</html>

Today's News:
1. It is a long established fact that a reader will be distracted by the readable content of a page when looking at its layout. The point of using Lorem Ipsum is that it has a more-or-less normal distribution of letters, as opposed to using 'Content here, content here', making it look like readable English. Many desktop publishing

packages and web page editors now use Lorem Ipsum as their default model text, and a search for 'lorem ipsum' will uncover many web sites still in their infancy. Various versions have evolved over the years, sometimes by accident, sometimes on purpose (injected humour and the like).

2. It is a long established fact that a reader will be distracted by the readable content of a page when looking at its layout. The point of using Lorem Ipsum is that it has a more-or-less normal distribution of letters, as opposed to using 'Content here, content here', making it look like readable English. Many desktop publishing packages and web page editors now use Lorem Ipsum as their default model text, and a search for 'lorem ipsum' will uncover many web sites still in their infancy. Various versions have evolved over the years, sometimes by accident, sometimes on purpose (injected humour and the like). 3. It is a long established fact that a reader will be distracted by the readable content of a page when looking at its layout. The point of using Lorem Ipsum is that it has a more-or-less normal distribution of letters, as opposed to using 'Content here, content here', making it look like readable English. Many desktop publishing packages and web page editors now use Lorem Ipsum as their default model text, and a search for 'lorem ipsum' will uncover many web sites still in their infancy. Various versions have evolved

over the years, sometimes by accident, sometimes on purpose (injected humour and the like).

Live Preview

Exercise 1

Download the Exercise 1

Exercise 1:

Create one HTML page and write the Headings 1 to 3 and under

each Heading write a paragraph of text.

LIVE PREVIEW

Exercise 2

DOWNLOAD THE EXERCISE 2 Exercise 2: Create one HTML page and write the Headings 1 and some

paragraph under it. Then draw a line under it and then show some more text.

Live Preview

3.5 – Single Line Break

Usage of Line Breaks

Line Breaks helps to break the link like the new line (\r\n) we have in the normal text file.

Breaks are used when we want to break a running line and start a new line. The more breaks you have the more new lines are added.

TAG:

ELEMENT:

 is a self-enclosing tags.

Sample Example

DOWNLOAD THE EXAMPLE

```
<!DOCTYPE html>
<html>
<head>
<meta charset="utf-8">
<meta name="viewport" content="width=device-width, initial-scale=1.0">
<meta name="description" content="Page Description">
<title>Line Break</title>
</head>
<body>
<!-- Observe how the data is organized with new line and empty spaces -->
<!-- <br> and <hr> are self closing tags -->
<h1>Today's News</h1> <p>1. It is a long established fact that a reader will be distracted by the readable content of a page when looking at its layout. <br> The point of using Lorem Ipsum is that it has a more-or-less normal distribution of letters, as opposed to using 'Content here, content here', making it look like readable English. Many desktop publishing packages and web page editors now use Lorem Ipsum as their default model text, and a search for 'lorem ipsum' will uncover many web sites still in their infancy. Various versions have evolved over the years, sometimes by accident, sometimes on purpose (injected humour and the like).</p>
<br>
<hr>
```

<p>2. It is a long established fact that a reader will be distracted by the readable content of a page when looking at its layout.

 The point of using Lorem Ipsum is that it has a more-or-less normal distribution of letters, as opposed to using 'Content here, content here', making it look like readable English. Many desktop publishing packages and web page editors now use Lorem Ipsum as their default model text, and a search for 'lorem ipsum' will uncover many web sites still in their infancy. Various versions have evolved over the years, sometimes by accident, sometimes on purpose (injected humour and the like).</p>

<hr>

<p>3. It is a long established fact that a reader will be distracted by the readable content of a page when looking at its layout.

 The point of using Lorem Ipsum is that it has a more-or-less normal distribution of letters, as opposed to using 'Content here, content here', making it look like readable English. Many desktop publishing packages and web page editors now use Lorem Ipsum as their default model text, and a search for 'lorem ipsum' will uncover many web sites still in their infancy. Various versions have evolved over the years, sometimes by accident, sometimes on purpose (injected humour and the like).</p>

</body>

</html>

Today's News:

1. It is a long established fact that a reader will be distracted by the readable content of a page when looking at its layout.

The point of using Lorem Ipsum is that it has a more-or-less normal distribution of letters, as opposed to using 'Content here, content here', making it look like readable English. Many desktop publishing packages and web page editors now use Lorem Ipsum as their default model text, and a search for 'lorem ipsum' will uncover many web sites still in their infancy. Various versions have evolved over the years, sometimes by accident, sometimes on purpose (injected humour and the like).

2. It is a long established fact that a reader will be distracted by the readable content of a page when looking at its layout.

The point of using Lorem Ipsum is that it has a more-or-less normal distribution of letters, as opposed to using 'Content here, content here', making it look like readable English. Many desktop publishing packages and web page editors now use Lorem Ipsum as their default model text, and a search for 'lorem ipsum' will uncover many web sites still in their infancy. Various versions have evolved over the years, sometimes by accident, sometimes on purpose (injected humour and the like).

3. It is a long established fact that a reader will be distracted by the readable content of a page when looking at its layout.

The point of using Lorem Ipsum is that it has a more-or-less normal distribution of letters, as opposed to using 'Content here, content here', making it look like readable English. Many desktop publishing packages and web page editors now use Lorem Ipsum as their default model text, and a search for 'lorem ipsum' will uncover many web sites still in their infancy. Various versions have evolved over the years, sometimes by accident, sometimes on purpose (injected humour and the like),

Live Preview

Exercise 1

Download the Exercise 1

Exercise 1:

Create one HTML page and add break line in the headings 1

LIVE PREVIEW

Exercise 2

DOWNLOAD THE EXERCISE 2

Exercise 2: Create one HTML page and break the paragraph line by line up to

10 lines.

LIVE PREVIEW

3.6 – Strong Text

Usage of Strong

Strong tag helps to bold the text and highlight the text to emphasis some line in the paragraph.

It is often used in the Paragraphs.
TAG: <strong>
ELEMENT: <strong>something</strong>
Sample Example
DOWNLOAD THE EXAMPLE

```
<!DOCTYPE html>
<html>
<head>
<meta charset="utf-8">
<meta name="viewport" content="width=device-width, initial-scale=1.0">
<meta name="description" content="Page Description">
<title>Strong</title>
</head>
<body>
<!-- Observe how the data is organized -->
<h1>Today's News</h1>
<p>1. "<strong>Lorem</strong> ipsum dolor sit amet, consectetur adipisicing elit, sed do eiusmod tempor incididunt ut labore et dolore magna aliqua. Ut enim ad minim veniam, quis nostrud exercitation ullamco laboris nisi ut aliquip ex ea commodo consequat. Duis aute irure dolor in reprehenderit in voluptate velit esse cillum dolore eu fugiat nulla pariatur. Excepteur sint occaecat cupidatat non proident, sunt in culpa qui officia deserunt mollit anim id est laborum."</p>
<p>2. "<strong>Lorem ipsum</strong> dolor sit amet, consectetur adipisicing elit, sed do eiusmod
```

tempor incididunt ut labore et dolore magna aliqua. Ut enim ad minim veniam, quis nostrud exercitation ullamco laboris nisi ut aliquip ex ea commodo consequat. Duis aute irure dolor in reprehenderit in voluptate velit esse cillum dolore eu fugiat nulla pariatur. Excepteur sint occaecat cupidatat non proident, sunt in culpa qui officia deserunt mollit anim id est laborum."</p>
<p>3. "<strong>Lorem ipsum dolor</strong> sit amet, consectetur adipisicing elit, sed do eiusmod tempor incididunt ut labore et dolore magna aliqua. Ut enim ad minim veniam, quis nostrud exercitation ullamco laboris nisi ut aliquip ex ea commodo consequat. Duis aute irure dolor in reprehenderit in voluptate velit esse cillum dolore eu fugiat nulla pariatur. Excepteur sint occaecat cupidatat non proident, sunt in culpa qui officia deserunt mollit anim id est laborum."</p>

Chapter 6: Embed Contents

Purpose of Embed Tags

Embed tags are used to include external resource into the html page. These resources could be in your server or located at some other location.

• Well, the main purpose of WWW was to connect all the contents together with a link and that makes the web so powerful that it has ability to connect things all over the web.

This concept makes the whole web very powerful.

• Here are the list of things you can embed in the HTML Page:

- Image
- Image with Attributes
- Image with Article
- Audio
- Video
- Embed one Page into Another (iFrame)
- Link Pages
- Anchor Links in the same page

These concepts will give you good idea on how to build your web page by combining the different components together.

Till now we have been working on writing text on the HTML page but in this section you will learn how to embed objects like image, audio or video on the page.

7.1 – Embed Image

Usage of Embed Image

<img> tag is used to embed image in the html page. The image could be in the same server or it could be in the different server location.

Good example could be the images you see on this page is coming up from the server and embedded into this page with the <img> tag.

TAG: <img>

ELEMENT: <img src="location" />

src – is an attribute of img tag and point to the location of the image file.

Sample Example

DOWNLOAD THE EXAMPLE

```
<!DOCTYPE html>
<html>
<head>
<meta charset="utf-8">
<meta name="viewport" content="width=device-width, initial-scale=1.0">
<meta name="description" content="Page Description">
<title>Embedded Image</title>
</head>
<body> <h1>German Shepherd</h1>
<img src ="dog1.jpg" alt="German Shepherd" >
<p>The German Shepherd (German: Deutscher Schäferhund, German pronunciation: is a breed of medium to large-sized working dog that originated in Germany. The breed's officially
```

```
recognized name is German Shepherd Dog in the English language (sometimes abbreviated as GSD). The breed was once known as the Alsatian in Britain and Ireland.[5] The German Shepherd is a relatively new breed of dog, with their origin dating to 1899. As part of the Herding Group, German Shepherds are working dogs developed originally for herding sheep. </p>
<hr>
<h1>Vacation Time!</h1>
<img src="https://i.imgur.com/xtoLyW2.jpg">
</body>
</html>
```

German Shepherd:

The German Shepherd (German: Deutscher Schäferhund, German pronunciation: is a breed of medium to large-sized working dog that originated in Germany. The breed's officially recognized name is German Shepherd Dog in the English language (sometimes abbreviated as GSD). The breed was once known as the Alsatian in Britain and Ireland.[5] The German Shepherd is a relatively new breed of dog, with their origin dating to 1899. As part of the Herding Group, German Shepherds are working dogs developed originally for herding sheep.

Vacation Time!

LIVE PREVIEW

Exercise 1

DOWNLOAD THE EXERCISE 1

Exercise 1: Put two images side by side in a table format. LIVE PREVIEW

7.2 – Embed Image with Attributes

Usage of Embed Image with Attributes

<img> tag has some attributes that can help to

resize the image

control the position of the image

Align text beside it

Alternative text to display when image is not loaded properly

Good example could be the size of the image you can specify the image height and width with the attribute.

alt attribute is displayed when image is not shown properly or missing. This also helps to show as a tool tip when you hover over the image.

TAG: <img>

ELEMENT: <img src="location" width="643" height="389" alt ="Hover on me" />

width– specifies the width of the image.

height– specifies the height of the image.

alt– specifies the alternative text of that image. Displays this text when image cannot be loaded.

Sample Example

Download the Example

```
<!DOCTYPE html>
<html>
```

```
<head>
<meta charset="utf-8">
<meta name="viewport" content="width=device-width, initial-scale=1.0">
<meta name="description" content="Page Description">
<title>Image Attributes</title>
</head>
<body>
<h1>German Shepherd</h1> <img src ="dog1.jpg" alt="This is alt text displayed for missing image" height="256" width="256 ">
<p>The German Shepherd (German: Deutscher Schäferhund, German pronunciation: is a breed of medium to large-sized working dog that originated in Germany. The breed's officially recognized name is German Shepherd Dog in the English language (sometimes abbreviated as GSD). The breed was once known as the Alsatian in Britain and Ireland.[5] The German Shepherd is a relatively new breed of dog, with their origin dating to 1899. As part of the Herding Group, German Shepherds are working dogs developed originally for herding sheep. </p>
<hr>
<h1><img src="https://i.imgur.com/xtoLyW2.jpg" height="128" width="128"> Vacation Time!</h1>
<hr>
</body>
</html>
```

German Shepherd

The German Shepherd (German: Deutscher Schäferhund, German pronunciation: is a breed of medium to large-sized working dog that originated in Germany. The breed's officially recognized name is German Shepherd Dog in the English language (sometimes abbreviated as GSD). The breed was once known as the Alsatian in Britain and Ireland.[5] The German Shepherd is a relatively new breed of dog, with their origin dating to 1899. As part of the Herding Group, German Shepherds are working dogs developed originally for herding sheep.

Live Preview

Exercise 1

Download the Exercise 1

Exercise 1:

Display images in small thumbnails (Width: 64 x Height: 64)

LIVE PREVIEW

Exercise 2

DOWNLOAD THE EXERCISE 2

Exercise 2: Make lines with Images Horizontal and Vertical. LIVE PREVIEW

7.3 – Embed Image in the Article

Usage of Embed Image in Article

<figure> is element inside the article that lets you define a image properly with a <figcaption> caption as well.

TAG: <figure>, <figcaption>

ELEMENT:

```
<article>
<figure>
<img src =”dog1.jpg” alt=”German Shepherd” height=”256” width=”256”> </article>
```

Sample Example

DOWNLOAD THE EXAMPLE

```
<!DOCTYPE html>
<html>
<head>
<meta charset="utf-8">
<meta name="viewport" content="width=device-width, initial-scale=1.0">
<meta name="description" content="Page Description">
<title>Image Article</title>
</head>
<body>
<section>
<article>
<header><h2>German Shepherd</h2></header>
<figure>
<img src ="dog1.jpg" alt="German Shepherd" height="256" width="256">
<p>The German Shepherd (German: Deutscher Schäferhund, German pronunciation: is a breed of medium to large-sized working dog that originated in Germany. The breed's officially recognized name is German Shepherd Dog in the English language (sometimes abbreviated as GSD). The breed was once known as the Alsatian
```

in Britain and Ireland.[5] The German Shepherd is a relatively new breed of dog, with their origin dating to 1899. As part of the Herding Group, German Shepherds are working dogs developed originally for herding sheep. </p>

<footer>True friend!</footer>

</article>

</section>

</body>

</html>

German Shepherd

Best bread in Dog Family

The German Shepherd (German: Deutscher Schäferhund, German pronunciation: is a breed of medium to large-sized working dog that originated in Germany. The breed's officially recognized name is German Shepherd Dog in the English language (sometimes abbreviated as GSD). The breed was once known as the Alsatian in Britain and Ireland.[5] The German Shepherd is a relatively new breed of dog, with their origin dating to 1899. As part of the Herding Group, German Shepherds are working dogs developed originally for herding sheep.

True friend!

Live Preview

Exercise 1

Download the Exercise 1

Exercise 1: Write Two Articles side by side like below.

Live Preview

Exercise 2

Download the Exercise 2

Exercise 2: Add thumbnail images in the Article.

Live Preview

7.4 – Embed Audio

Usage of Embed Audio

<audio> elements are used to embed audio files in the html page.

TAG: <audio>

ELEMENT:

```
<audio controls autoplay>
<source src=”dogbarking.mp3” type=”audio/mpeg”>
The browser does not support this audio format.
</audio>
```

autoplay – This attribute of Audio helps to play the audio automatically

controls – This attribute of Audio helps to show the audio controls.

Sample Example

Download the Example

```
<!DOCTYPE html>
<html>
<head>
<meta charset="utf-8">
<meta name="viewport" content="width=device-width, initial-scale=1.0">
<meta name="description" content="Page Description">
<title>Audio Example</title>
```

```
</head>
<body>
<section>
<article>
<header><h2>German Shepherd</h2></header>
<figure>
<img src ="dog1.jpg" alt="German Shepherd"
height="256" width="256">
<figcaption>Best bread in Dog
Family</figcaption>
</figure>
<div>
<p> <audio controls>
<source src="dog-barking.mp3"
type="audio/mpeg">
Having issue with the Audio?
</audio>
</p>
</div>
<p>The German Shepherd (German: Deutscher
Schäferhund, German pronunciation: is a breed of
medium to large-sized working dog that
originated in Germany. The breed's officially
recognized name is German Shepherd Dog in the
English language (sometimes abbreviated as
GSD). The breed was once known as the Alsatian
in Britain and Ireland.[5] The German Shepherd is
a relatively new breed of dog, with their origin
dating to 1899. As part of the Herding Group,
German Shepherds are working dogs developed
originally for herding sheep. </p>
```

```
<footer>True friend!</footer>
</article>
</section>
</body>
</html>
```

German Shepherd:

The German Shepherd (German: Deutscher Schäferhund, German pronunciation: is a breed of medium to large-sized working dog that originated in Germany. The breed's officially recognized name is German Shepherd Dog in the English language (sometimes abbreviated as GSD). The breed was once known as the Alsatian in Britain and Ireland.[5] The German Shepherd is a relatively new breed of dog, with their origin dating to 1899. As part of the Herding Group, German Shepherds are working dogs developed originally for herding sheep.

True friend!

Exercise 1

Download the Exercise 1

Exercise 1: Embed two Audio files in the same page. Live Preview

7.5 – Embed Video

Usage of Embed Video

<video> elements are used to embed video files in the html page.

TAG: <video>

ELEMENT:

```
<video width="320" height="240" controls>
<source src="Dog.mp4" type="video/mp4">
Having issue with the Video?
</video>
```

controls – This attribute of Video helps to show the video controls.

Sample Example

Download the Example

```
<!DOCTYPE html>
<html>
<head>
<meta charset="utf-8">
<meta name="viewport" content="width=device-width, initial-scale=1.0">
<meta name="description" content="Page Description">
<title>Video Example</title>
</head>
<body>
<section>
<article>
<header><h2>German Shepherd</h2></header>
<figure> <img src ="dog1.jpg" alt="German Shepherd" height="256" width="256">
<figcaption>Best bread in Dog Family</figcaption>
</figure>
<div>
<p>
<video width="320" height="240" controls>
```

```
<source src="Dog.mp4" type="video/mp4">
Having issue with the Video?
</video>
</p>
</div>
<p>The German Shepherd (German: Deutscher Schäferhund, German pronunciation: is a breed of medium to large-sized working dog that originated in Germany. The breed's officially recognized name is German Shepherd Dog in the English language (sometimes abbreviated as GSD). The breed was once known as the Alsatian in Britain and Ireland.[5] The German Shepherd is a relatively new breed of dog, with their origin dating to 1899. As part of the Herding Group, German Shepherds are working dogs developed originally for herding sheep. </p>
<footer>True friend!</footer>
</article>
</section> </body>
</html>
```

German Shepherd:

The German Shepherd (German: Deutscher Schäferhund, German pronunciation: is a breed of medium to large-sized working dog that originated in Germany. The breed's officially recognized name is German Shepherd Dog in the English language (sometimes abbreviated as GSD). The breed was once known as the Alsatian in Britain and Ireland. [5] The German Shepherd is a relatively new breed of dog, with their origin dating to 1899. As part of the Herding Group, German Shepherds are working dogs developed originally for herding sheep.

True friend!

Exercise 1

Download the Exercise 1

Exercise 1: Embed Two Video files in the same page. Separate them with line.

LIVE PREVIEW

Exercise 2

DOWNLOAD THE EXERCISE 2

Exercise 2: Hide all the controls of the Video. Do not delete the Video tag but hide it.

7.6 – Embed iFrame

Usage of Embed Frame

<iframe> tags are used to embed other html page inside the existing one.

TAG: <iframe>

ELEMENT:

```
<iframe src="iframesample.html" height="300"></iframe>
```

Sample Example

Download the Example

```
<!DOCTYPE html>
<html>
<head>
<meta charset="utf-8">
<meta name="viewport" content="width=device-width, initial-scale=1.0">
```

```
<meta name="description" content="Page Description">
<title>iFrame Example</title> </head>
<body>
<iframe src="iframe-sample.html" height="300"></iframe>
</body>
</html>
```

Exercise 1

Download the Exercise 1

Exercise 1: Embed two file into 1 HTML page one after the other.

LIVE PREVIEW

Exercise 2

DOWNLOAD THE EXERCISE 2

Exercise 2: Show the iframe side by side.

LIVE PREVIEW

7.7 – Embed Links

Usage of Embed Links

<a> tag allows you to link other pages, images, audio or video file or any other url using the <a> tag.

This is the most powerful and important tag in HTML that you will be using alot.

TAG: <a>

ELEMENT: <a href="location" />

target – This attribute decides where the link should open

target = "_blank" – Will open the link in another window

Sample Example

Download the Example

```
<!DOCTYPE html>
<html>
<head>
<meta charset="utf-8">
<meta name="viewport" content="width=device-width, initial-scale=1.0">
<meta name="description" content="Page Description">
<title>Hyperlink Example</title>
</head>
<body>
<h1>Hyperlink Example</h1>
<a href="https://www.google.com">Open Google.com Site Here.</a>
<br>
<a href="https://www.google.com" target="_blank">Open Google.com Site in New Window.</a>
</body>
</html>
```

LIVE PREVIEW

Exercise 1

DOWNLOAD THE EXERCISE 1

Exercise 1: Put a link to another page from existing page. Back to the old page.

LIVE PREVIEW

Exercise 2

DOWNLOAD THE EXERCISE 2 Exercise 2: Create 1 link that opens the image into another page.

Live Preview

7.8 – Embed Anchor

Usage of Embed Anchor

<a> tag allows you to link to the specific section of the page.

Anchors helps users to jump on the specific section of the same page.

id – This id attribute is first assigned to the tag to mark as a anchor.

Using <a> tag, we can provide link to that specific location of the page.

TAG: <a>

ELEMENT:

<h1 id=”location1”>

<a href=”#location1”>Go Location 1</a>

Sample Example

Download the Example

```
<!DOCTYPE html>
<html>
<head>
<meta charset="utf-8">
<meta name="viewport" content="width=device-width, initialscale=1.<br>0">
<meta name="description" content="Page Description">
<title>Hyperlink Example</title>
</head>
<body>
<h1 id="top">Hyperlink Example</h1>
<div >
```

<p>

What is Lorem Ipsum?

Lorem Ipsum is simply dummy text of the printing and typesetting industry.
 Lorem Ipsum has been the industry's standard dummy text ever since the 1500s, when an unknown printer took a galley of type and scrambled it to make a type specimen book.
 It has survived not only five centuries, but also the leap into electronic typesetting, remaining essentially unchanged.
 It was popularised in the 1960s with the release of Letraset sheets containing Lorem Ipsum passages, and more recently with desktop publishing software like Aldus PageMaker including versions of Lorem Ipsum.

Why do we use it?

It is a long established fact that a reader will be distracted by the readable content of a page when looking at its layout.
 The point of using Lorem Ipsum is that it has a more-or-less normal distribution of letters, as opposed to using 'Content here, content here', making it look like readable English.
 Many desktop publishing packages and web page editors now use Lorem Ipsum as their default model text, and a search for 'lorem ipsum' will uncover many web sites still in their infancy.
 Various versions have evolved over the years, sometimes by accident, sometimes on purpose (injected humour and the like).

Where does it come from?
Contrary to popular belief, Lorem Ipsum is not simply random text.
 It has roots in a piece of classical Latin literature from 45 BC, making it over 2000 years old.
 Richard McClintock, a Latin professor at Hampden-Sydney College in Virginia, looked up one of the more obscure Latin words, consectetur, from a Lorem Ipsum passage, and going through the cites of the word in classical literature, discovered the undoubtable source.
 Lorem Ipsum comes from sections 1.
10.
32 and 1.
10.
33 of "de Finibus Bonorum et Malorum" (The Extremes of Good and Evil) by Cicero, written in 45 BC.
 This book is a treatise on the theory of ethics, very popular during the Renaissance.
 The first line of Lorem Ipsum, "Lorem ipsum dolor sit amet.
.
", comes from a line in section 1.
10.
32.
The standard chunk of Lorem Ipsum used since the 1500s is reproduced below for those interested.
 Sections 1.
10.
32 and 1.
10.
33 from "de Finibus Bonorum et Malorum" by Cicero are also reproduced in their exact original form, accompanied by English versions from the 1914 translation by H.
 Rackham.
</p>
<p>
What is Lorem Ipsum?

Lorem Ipsum is simply dummy text of the printing and typesetting industry.
 Lorem Ipsum has been the industry's standard dummy text ever since the 1500s, when an unknown printer took a galley of type and scrambled it to make a type specimen book.
 It has survived not only five centuries, but also the leap into electronic typesetting, remaining essentially unchanged.
 It was popularised in the 1960s with the release of Letraset sheets containing Lorem Ipsum passages, and more recently with desktop publishing software like Aldus PageMaker including versions of Lorem Ipsum.

Why do we use it?

It is a long established fact that a reader will be distracted by the readable content of a page when looking at its layout.
 The point of using Lorem Ipsum is that it has a more-or-less normal distribution of letters, as opposed to using 'Content here, content here', making it look like readable English.
 Many desktop publishing packages and web page editors now use Lorem Ipsum as their default model text, and a search for 'lorem ipsum' will uncover many web sites still in their infancy.
 Various versions have evolved over the years, sometimes by accident, sometimes on purpose (injected humour and the like).

Where does it come from?

Contrary to popular belief, Lorem Ipsum is not simply random text.
 It has roots in a piece of classical Latin literature from 45 BC, making it over 2000 years old.
 Richard McClintock, a Latin professor at HampdenSydney College in Virginia, looked up one of the more obscure Latin words, consectetur, from a Lorem Ipsum passage, and going through the cites of the word in classical literature, discovered the undoubtable source.
 Lorem Ipsum comes from sections 1.
10.
32 and 1.
10.
33 of "de Finibus Bonorum et Malorum" (The Extremes of Good and Evil) by Cicero, written in 45 BC.
 This book is a treatise on the theory of ethics, very popular during the Renaissance.
 The first line of Lorem Ipsum, "Lorem ipsum dolor sit amet.
.
", comes from a line in section 1.
10.
32.

The standard chunk of Lorem Ipsum used since the 1500s is reproduced below for those interested.
 Sections 1.
10.
32 and 1.
10.
33 from "de Finibus Bonorum et Malorum" by Cicero are also reproduced in their exact original form, accompanied by English versions from the 1914 translation by H.
 Rackham.

</p>

</div>

<a href="#top">Go Top</a>

</body> </html>

Exercise 1
Download the Exercise 1
Exercise 1: Create 5 Anchor points in the page.
Live Preview

8. FORMS

8 FORMS

Purpose of Form Elements

Form elements are the basic building blocks of HTML page. This is most common elements that you will be using for any website development project.

Common scenario where you will use form elements:

Contact Form
Newsletter Form
Register or Login Form
Personal Information Form

Forms are used to collect information from the user and post the data to the script running on the server.

The script on the server can save the data in the database or file.

With forms, you can restrict the data submit to the server and use different form elements to capture different type of data from user. Like you can collect email id, phone number or Date from the form.

Here are the list of Form Elements which are most commonly used:

- Basic Form Elements
- Input Elements
- Select Element • Checkboxes
- Text Area
- Other Form Elements
- Form Action – GET
- Form Action – POST
- Radio Buttons

Learning how to work with the form elements can help you build a form on the web page that capture the data from the user.

Remember, Forms are used to capture data from user and post them to script running on the server which might take action on the data.

8.1 – Basic Form Elements

Usage of Basic Form Elements

Form tag are used to define all the form elements and into which users enter the data and submit the data to the user.

To capture the user data, we define form and all the elements depending on the type of the data to be captured from the user.

All the form elements should be defined inside the <form> tag.

TAG: <form>

ELEMENT:

```
<form>
<input type="text" id="input_name" >
<input type="submit">
```

<input type="reset"> </form>

id – is an attribute that can used to identify that element in the HTML page.

In the Example below,

<label for="input_name">Label for Input Box:</label>

<input id ="input_name" type="text" placeholder="Placeholder">

label is used to enter some text before the input field.

for attribute in label indicates the label is for which input tag.

input tag is used to define type of the field with the type field.

type attribute value is “text” which indicates that is a text box.

placeholder attribute shows a small text in the box to indicate what to type

Sample Example

Download the Example

```
<!DOCTYPE html>
<html>
<head>
<meta charset="utf-8">
<meta name="viewport" content="width=device-width, initial-scale=1.0">
<meta name="description" content="Page Description">
<title>Form Elements</title>
</head> <body>
<h1>Form Basic Elements</h1>
```

```
<form>
<label for="input_name">Label for Input
Box:</label>
<input id ="input_name" type="text"
placeholder="Placeholder">
<p><input type="submit"> <input
type="reset"></p>
</form>
<hr>
<h1>Student Information Form</h1>
<form>
<p>
<label for="input_name">Full Name:</label>
<input id ="input_name" type="text"
placeholder="Name here">
</p>
<p>
<label for="input_age">Age:</label>
<input id ="input_age" type="text"
placeholder="Your Age">
</p>
<p>
<label for="input_hobbies">Hobbies:</label>
<input id ="input_hobbies" type="text"
placeholder="Seperate Hobbies with ,">
</p>
<p><input type="submit" value="Send"> <input
type="reset" value="Clear"></p>
</form>
</body>
</html> Form Basic Elements:
```

Student Information Form:

Live Preview

Exercise 1

Download the Exercise 1

Exercise 1: Create a form like this below Live Preview

8.2 – Input Box Form Elements

Usage of Input Box Form Element

<input> tag elements are used to display text box, submit buttons, email boxes and many other types of form elements.

input tags are defined inside the form elements.

TAG: <input>, <fieldset>, <legend>, <form>

ELEMENT:

```
<form>
<fieldset>
<legend>Input Fields</legend>
<input type="text" id="input_name" >
<input type="submit">
<input type="reset">
</fieldset>
</form>
```

fieldset tag is used to group the elements together.

legend tag is used to display short heading of group of elements for readability purpose.

id – is an attribute used to identify an element or give a reference name to it.

type is an attribute used to indicate that input type is text or submit or reset button.

Sample Example

Download the Example

```
<!DOCTYPE html>
<html>
<head>
<meta charset="utf-8">
<meta name="viewport" content="width=device-
width, initial-scale=1.0">
<meta    name="description"    content="Page
Description"> <title>Form Elements</title>
</head>
<body>
<h1>Form Basic Elements</h1>
<form>
<fieldset>
<legend>Input Box Elements</legend>
<p>
<label for="input_text">Text:</label>
<input    id    ="input_text"    type="text"
placeholder="Text">
</p>
<p>
<label for="input_email">Email:</label>
<input    id    ="input_email"    type="email"
placeholder="test@domain.com">
</p>
<p>
<label for="input_password">Password:</label>
<input  id  ="input_password"  type="password"
placeholder="Password">
</p> <p>
<label for="input_number">Number:</label>
```

```
<input id ="input_number" type="number" placeholder="Number">
</p>
<p>
<label for="input_phonenumber">Phone Number:</label>
<input id ="input_phonenumber" type="tel" placeholder="(999) 999999">
</p>
<p>
<label for="input_url">URL:</label>
<input id ="input_url" type="url" placeholder="http://somesite.com">
</p>
<p>
<label for="input_search">Search:</label>
<input id ="input_search" type="search" placeholder="Search...">
</p>
</fieldset>
<p><input type="submit"> <input type="reset"></p>
</form>
<hr> <h1>Student Information Form</h1>
<form>
<p>
<label for="input_name">Full Name:</label>
<input id ="input_name" type="text" placeholder="Name here">
</p>
<p>
```

```
<label for="input_age">Age:</label>
<input id ="input_age" type="number" placeholder="Your Age">
</p>
<p>
<label for="input_hobbies">Email ID:</label>
<input id ="input_hobbies" type="email" placeholder="Email ID">
</p>
<p><input type="submit" value="Send"> <input type="reset" value="Clear"></p>
</form>
</body>
</html>
```

LIVE PREVIEW

Exercise 1

DOWNLOAD THE EXERCISE 1

Exercise 1: Use FieldSet and Legend around the Personal Information Form. LIVE PREVIEW:

8.3 – Select Form Elements

Usage of Select Form Element

<select> Form elements are used to show list of values that user can select from.

☐ It is like asking user to select one from the option given.

TAG: <select>, <option>, <optgroup>

ELEMENT:

☐ <form>

☐ <select>

□ □10″>
□ <option>1</option>
□ <option>2</option>
□ </optgroup>
□ </select>
□ </form>

optgroup will group the options together with a label.

Sample Example

Download the Example

```
<!DOCTYPE html>
<html>
<head>
<meta charset="utf-8">
<meta name="viewport" content="width=device-width, initial-scale=1.0">
<meta name="description" content="Page Description">
<title>Form Elements</title>
</head>
<body>
<h1>Form Basic Elements</h1>
<form>
<fieldset>
<legend>Input Box Elements</legend>
<p>
<label for="input_text">Text:</label>
<input id ="input_text" type="text" placeholder="Text">
</p> <p>
<label for="input_email">Email:</label>
```

```
<input id ="input_email" type="email"
placeholder="test@domain.com">
</p>
<p>
<label for="input_password">Password:</label>
<input id ="input_password" type="password"
placeholder="Password">
</p>
<p>
<label for="input_number">Number:</label>
<input id ="input_number" type="number"
placeholder="Number">
</p>
<p>
<label for="input_phonenumber">Phone
Number:</label>
<input id ="input_phonenumber" type="tel"
placeholder="(999) 999999">
</p>
<p>
<label for="input_url">URL:</label> <input id
="input_url" type="url"
placeholder="http://somesite.com">
</p>
<p>
<label for="input_search">Search:</label>
<input id ="input_search" type="search"
placeholder="Search...">
</p>
</fieldset>
<fieldset>
```

```
<legend>Select Form Element</legend>
<p>
<label for="select">Select</label>
<select id="select">
<optgroup label="Option Group 1">
<option>Option1 One</option>
<option>Option1 Two</option>
<option>Option1 Three</option>
</optgroup>
<optgroup label="Option Group 2">
<option>Option2 One</option>
<option>Option2                    Two</option>
<option>Option2 Three</option>
</optgroup>
</select>
</p>
</fieldset>
<p><input          type="submit">          <input
type="reset"></p>
</form>
<hr>
<h1>Student Information Form</h1>
<form>
<p>
<label for="input_name">Full Name:</label>
<input     id     ="input_name"     type="text"
placeholder="Name here">
</p>
<p>
<label for="input_age">Age:</label>
```

```
<input id ="input_age" type="number"
placeholder="Your Age">
</p>
<p>
<label for="input_hobbies">Email ID:</label>
<input id ="input_hobbies" type="email"
placeholder="Email ID">
</p>
<p>
<label for="input_mobile">Mobile No.:</label>
<input id ="input_mobile" type="tel"
placeholder="Contact Number">
</p>
<p>
<label for="select_class">Applying for</label>
<select id="select_class">
<optgroup label="Primary">
<option>1</option>
<option>2</option>
<option>3</option>
<option>4</option>
<option>5</option>
<option>6</option>
<option>7</option>
</optgroup>
<optgroup label="Secondary">
<option>8</option>
<option>9</option>
<option>10</option>
</optgroup>
</select>
```

```
</p>
<p><input type="submit" value="Send"> <input type="reset" value="Clear"></p>
</form>
</body>
</html>
```

LIVE PREVIEW

Exercise 1

DOWNLOAD THE EXERCISE 1

Exercise 1: Show Select group 1-10 values with 1-10 as header and A-D as
group header with A-D options in the form.

LIVE PREVIEW

Exercise 2

DOWNLOAD THE EXERCISE 2

Exercise 2: Show all the months in the select element. LIVE PREVIEW

8.4 – Radio Buttons Form Elements

Usage of Radio Buttons

Radio buttons are used to give options for user to pick one option from the various options provided.

User can only select one from the options

TAG: <input>

ELEMENT:

```
<form>
<input id ="radio1" name="gender" type="radio" checked>
<input id ="radio2" name="gender" type="radio">
```

```
</form>
```

☐ type = radio will change the input type to radio button. ☐ checked attribute will select the radio button.

Sample Example:

```
<!DOCTYPE html>
<html>
<head>
<meta charset="utf-8">
<meta name="viewport" content="width=device-width, initial-scale=1.0">
<meta name="description" content="Page Description">
<title>Form Elements</title>
</head>
<body>
<h1>Form Basic Elements</h1>
<form>
<fieldset>
<legend>Input Box Elements</legend>
<p>
<label for="input_text">Text:</label>
<input id ="input_text" type="text" placeholder="Text">
</p> <p>
<label for="input_email">Email:</label>
<input id ="input_email" type="email" placeholder="test@domain.com">
</p>
<p>
<label for="input_password">Password:</label>
```

```
<input id ="input_password" type="password"
placeholder="Password">
</p>
<p>
<label for="input_number">Number:</label>
<input id ="input_number" type="number"
placeholder="Number">
</p>
<p>
<label for="input_phonenumber">Phone
Number:</label>
<input id ="input_phonenumber" type="tel"
placeholder="(999) 999999">
</p>
<p>
<label for="input_url">URL:</label> <input id
="input_url" type="url"
placeholder="http://somesite.com">
</p>
<p>
<label for="input_search">Search:</label>
<input id ="input_search" type="search"
placeholder="Search...">
</p>
</fieldset>
<fieldset>
<legend>Select Form Element</legend>
<p>
<label for="select">Select</label>
<select id="select">
<optgroup label="Option Group 1">
```

```
<option>Option1 One</option>
<option>Option1 Two</option>
<option>Option1 Three</option>
</optgroup>
<optgroup label="Option Group 2">
<option>Option2 One</option>
<option>Option2 Two</option>
<option>Option2 Three</option>
</optgroup>
</select>
</p>
</fieldset>
<fieldset>
<legend>Radio Button Element</legend>
<p>
<ul>
<li>
<label for="radio_option1">Option 1:</label>
<input id ="radio_option1" name="radio"
type="radio" checked>
</li>
<li>
<label for="radio_option2">Option 2:</label>
<input id ="radio_option2" name="radio"
type="radio">
</li>
</ul>
</p>
</fieldset> <p><input type="submit"> <input
type="reset"></p>
</form>
```

```
<hr>
<h1>Student Information Form</h1>
<form>
<p>
<label for="input_name">Full Name:</label>
<input id ="input_name" type="text"
placeholder="Name here">
</p>
<p>
<label for="input_age">Age:</label>
<input id ="input_age" type="number"
placeholder="Your Age">
</p>
<p>
<label for="input_hobbies">Email ID:</label>
<input id ="input_hobbies" type="email"
placeholder="Email ID">
</p>
<p>
<label for="input_mobile">Mobile No.:</label>
<input id ="input_mobile" type="tel"
placeholder="Contact Number"> <p>
<label for="select_class">Applying for</label>
<select id="select_class">
<optgroup label="Primary">
<option>1</option>
<option>2</option>
<option>3</option>
<option>4</option>
<option>5</option>
<option>6</option>
```

```
<option>7</option>
</optgroup>
<optgroup label="Secondary">
<option>8</option>
<option>9</option>
<option>10</option>
</optgroup>
</select> <!-- Observe how the Radio buttons are
grouped with name attribute -->
<p>
<h3>Gender</h3>
<label for="radio_male">Male:</label>
<input id ="radio_male" name="gender"
type="radio" checked>
<label for="radio_female">Female:</label>
<input id ="radio_female" name="gender"
type="radio">
</p>
<p><input type="submit" value="Send"> <input
type="reset" value="Clear"></p>
</form>
</body>
</html>
```

Chapter 7: How Websites Are Created: Html, Css, Php And Javascript

Website, at the most basic level, consists of HTML code. HTML is a markup language, which is used in all websites. HTML controls how website should be displayed on web browser. HTML code contains text which is displayed on website; also, HTML can show images and tables on screen, among other functions. HTML code is saved as text file with .htm or .html extension. Learning HTML is easy and there are many full size books about HTML, but I will show you one practical example on how website is built using HTML for you to really understand how HTML works. Create new text document in your operating system, type text provided below and save it as example.html. Here is how to do this in Microsoft Windows operating system (Windows 7 was used in this example): right click mouse when pointer is hovered over Desktop or some other directory. Select New>Text Document. Hit Enter key to name file with default name (in my case it named "New Text Document"). Open newly created file using Notepad or any text editor software and type in text provided below:

image 1: code to be inserted in text file

Save file with text included with the name example.html; Note that .html extension is important as it marks the file as being HTML code file. Using Notepad, select File>Save As..., then in "File name" field type example.html and click Save. Now, new file named example.html should appear in current directory where you saved text file. When you open this file using web browser, something like this should appear:

image 2: file example.html opened in web browser

This is how this code is rendered using web browser. I used Mozilla Firefox browser but generally all browsers should display this similarly. Now let's discuss what each HTML code element does. First of all pay attention at <HTML> and </HTML> tags. Tags are used in HTML to mark some text and code to display it accordingly. <HTML> and </HTML> tags are required and all websites have them in their HTML code. Their purpose it to mark whole document as being HTML document. Every HTML code elements should be entered inside <HTML> and </HTML> tags. There are other tags as you might noticed, for example <p>, </p> and <b>, </b> among others. Every tag is either opening tag or closing tag. Opening tags denote the where the formatting starts of particular code or text snippet, whereas closing tag denotes the end of tag formatting. For example, code snippet <b> This text is bold.</b> makes text "This text is bold" bold when rendered using browser. Some tags are not used for text formatting, for example

<title> tag is used to display page title in browsers as you can see in image above. You can see where "Page title here" is displayed in browser: where webpage tab is, at the top. HTML has some rules also, for example you might wonder what are the purpose of <head> and <body> tags. These are tags HTML requires to have into HTML code. These tags don't have specific purpose, but some rules apply: <title> tag should be inside <head> tag and regular text of webpage should be in <body> tag. <p> tag is called paragraph tag and it makes text indented from other paragraph's text, like real world text paragraphs in books. <h> tag is called heading tag and it is used to mark particular text as heading. It is interesting that different browsers can possibly render text differently that is inside <h> tags, but generally all browsers render it as large text with different font than regular website text. You can insert several <p> tags inside <body> tags and construct website that way; then you can add images to websites using <img> tag, add tables and so on to construct website by coding yourself. But as I mentioned, this book will not cover all these technologies fully because there are full large books on these subjects and the aim of this book is to teach you several different ways to easily construct websites. If you want to learn basics of HTML, I would recommend HTML & CSS Design and Build Websites by Jon Duckett, which is very good quality, well structured book and is very

easy to read and understand compared to other books. I tried it myself and it was also number one bestseller at its category. But my advise is not to learn all the functions of HTML and don't waste too much time on that; instead, learn the basics and as you will read in this book there are many software and websites which generate HTML code for you themselves! So only the basic understanding of HTML will be generally enough, but in specific cases you can learn only the features needed. Sometimes, for example websites ask you to place some custom HTML code into your webpage; when you know how HTML works basically, you can easily do this. Generally, websites are collection of several .html files, images, videos, PHP code files and other media. When user visits webpage, index.html is loaded first. Them, index.html can link other .html files and graphics which will be loaded if needed. HTML5 is the latest version of HTML at this time of writing. It added many big changes to the previous version of HTML and now even has features to create programmable webpages with animation - so you can possibly create HTML5 game or similar application!
Now, what is CSS? CSS is an abbreviation for "Cascading Style Sheets" and it is the language used for setting specific elements of webpage, like what color of webpage background should be, how titles and paragraphs will appear (font, indentation) and other similar things. CSS is

basically a collection of rules for specific HTML elements. CSS files are text files which are saved in the .html file directory with an .css extension. Then, from .html file .css file is linked and it's rules are used. This is convenient because you can externally change how HTML objects will appear using .css file. Let's see how CSS practically works by example. Create new text file in the location where you saved example.html file you created earlier. Type this text in this file and save it as styles.css using the same method you saved example.html file.

image 3: code for file styles.css

Now, when you open example.html file, you should see same text and structure but with different colors. The color of background and heading has changed as you can see. This changes are caused by and are controlled using styles.css file. This is the basic principle of how CSS works. As you can see, you can write rules in CSS for HTML tags, for example CSS rule body {background-color: rgb(113,213,170);} means to change background color to RGB values 113, 213 and 170, respectively. RGB is an abbreviation for Red, Green, Blue. RGB is used to represent any color in digital images. Using the combination of red, green and blue lights any color can be produced on computer screen. Each red, green and blue value can be from 0 to 255. You can try different numbers to get different colors when webpage will be opened in web browser. The great thing is that you also don't need to learn all the features of CSS. You just need to know basics, as was the case with HTML. Many website creation software and web based website creators generate CSS automatically, which is great time saver for you. There are complete books about CSS, but mostly there are books that cover both HTML and CSS. Again, I would recommend book HTML & CSS Design and Build Websites by Jon Duckett to learn CSS and HTML. Now you might ask why CSS is needed if HTML also has formatting, color and style functions? The reality is that in the past, web designers created websites using only HTML, but later there was a need to distinguish from page structure page styles and CSS was created. It is also very convenient because you can separately control the visual appearance of webpage and don't touch to it's main structure. Every website consists of HTML code so it is main "skeleton" for websites. HTML contains all the text that website has, but CSS controls how this text appears (among other visual options). Because HTML contains all the real text that website uses, search engines like Google also use HTML to index website and make it searchable on the internet.

PHP is different language compared to HTML and CSS and it's purpose is different: rather than being a formatting language like HTML and CSS, PHP is a programming language which is used to write different kinds of web programs. Web programs can do many different things, like some calculations, generate dynamic webpages, generate content specific advertisements... They are like regular desktop computer programs which can do many interesting things based on user input. PHP is difficult to learn and write in compared to HTML and CSS, because you need to program and not just write CSS or HTML rules: which text should be bold, what color should be background an so on. PHP has conditions as regular programming languages have, for example if statements which define program flow based on specific condition, for example "if a > 5 then do command 1, otherwise do command 2". Other than this PHP has many commands which are also found in other computer programming languages. Writing PHP code is time consuming and requires thorough organization, but it is very powerful and adds dynamic features to HTML and CSS code. It is important to know that PHP is server side scripting (or programming) language. What this means is that PHP program is processed and works using web server (or just server), which is large and powerful computer which hosts website along with PHP codes; web server can also run PHP programs, it has RAM as regular computers and storage devices. PHP is mostly needed in cases when you want to create dynamic website or want to add website some programmable functionality. Web design studios use PHP to write customer ordered custom websites and charge very large amounts of money for this job. But the great thing for you is that there are many free CMS engines today using which you can create fully dynamic website without the knowledge of PHP and even without knowledge of HTML and CSS! You will learn about these CMS engines and WordPress - the most popular of those later in the book. Another difficulty in learning PHP is that you need to know HTML and CSS in advance to learn PHP - because PHP also programs how HTML and CSS elements should behave.

Javascript, on the other hand, is a client side programming language. Client side programming language means that programs written in javascript are processed and run using user's computer - using user's web browser (computer or other device which connects to server is called "client"). Javascript has many functions and it can add some dynamic features to website, but PHP is more powerful and also more difficult to learn and write. Javascript is often taught as first programming language for those who start to learn programming because of it's simplicity. Javascript also has if conditions and other features commonly found in programming languages. You can run and test javascript programs directly using your web browser. Javascript is generally taught earlier than PHP but after HTML and CSS. You can learn javascript to

add some functionalities to website but generally websites which use PHP can have same features. You can learn javascript in short time if you want using short books but generally it is needed to know HTML and CSS prior to learning javascript.
There are other technologies also, but those where the most common and essential to know. Later in the book I will use these terms (HTML, CSS, PHP...), so you'll know what I will mean.

Creating websites by coding yourself from scratch
This is the way most beginners choose to learn about website creation; this happens probably because this is the most natural way of creating websites – writing your own code. Also, another reason could be that many people are not just aware that there are other easier ways to create website other than writing your website code from scratch. Because of people mostly don't know about other alternative ways of creating websites, they buy large books to learn about website creation coding languages and technologies like HTML, CSS, PHP, JavaScript...
This way of creating websites has very big advantage (although it also has big disadvantages) – the control of every aspect of website, because you wrote all the code for the website, you should know what each code section does. You can customize your website in any way (if you have technical knowledge, of course) if you write it yourself. Another advantage is that you

will learn about inner workings of how websites work; if you can code websites yourself, you can also work as a web developer. Web developers make serious money by creating custom coded websites. Even with these advantages, I personally don't advice you to select this way of creating websites if you want to create websites with minimal resources and in shortest time possible, except if you want to work as an web developer, because of the following big disadvantages:

- It needs much time and resources to learn coding languages
- It is possible for hackers to exploit some security error in your code and possibly destroy or attack your website
- It needs much time to code your website on your own
- You have to learn about many different complex technologies and programming languages to create dynamic websites (PHP, JavaScript...)
- At minimum, you have to learn HTML and CSS for creating static websites

However, if you choose this method, you will need to spend some money on the following: domain name (about 15$/year) and hosting (about 4$ or more/month). Although you can write code in every plain text editor, such as Notepad which comes with Microsoft Windows, it is much convenient and acceptable to write code in specifically designed software for this task.

These software tools are called code editors. The most popular software in this category is Adobe Dreamweaver, but you can also use free, open source software Notepad++ to write code. The advantage of code editors is that they have many features which help you write code faster and efficiently without errors: they have code coloring ability to make certain code elements in different color to make code easier to read; they have code correction, type auto completion, auto indentation and many useful features for website coders. They also support many popular coding languages and technologies, like HTML, CSS, Javascript, PHP and others. Also, some of the code editors including Adobe Dreamweaver can display how your code will be rendered in browsers as you can see on the following image:

image 4: code as it will appear in web browsers (screenshot of Adobe Dreamweaver CS6)

In this image, you can see that "Split" mode is selected. This mode allows us to see both code (shown on the left side) and how it will be rendered in web browsers (shown on the right side). To conclude, creating websites by coding yourself if very time consuming and resource intensive task; it was the only way to create website in the past but not any more. Today there are much easier ways to create even fully dynamic website in several hours if not in shorter time!

Creating websites using WYSIWYG editor software

If you want to create professionally looking static websites in shortest time and most easily – by visually arranging graphics, text, buttons etc., then you can use WYSIWYG software. WYSIWYG (abbreviation for "What You See Is What You Get") is website editor software, which allows the creation of static websites by dragging and placing text, graphics and other objects to assemble webpages. Then, this individual webpages (.html file is generated for each webpage) are linked together by WYSIWYG software and one complete website is generated. The example of how WYSIWYG software works is provided on the image below. In this example, I captured Serif Webplus X8, one of the most popular and best WYSIWYG software in my opinion (I say this because I tested almost all other WYSIWYG editors).

image 5: Serif Webplus X8, WYSIWYG software which allows website creation by drag and dropping items

As you can see on this image, Serif Webplus X8 has different objects on the rightmost panel like text, image, table and other objects which can be easily dragged and arranged to visually construct website. On the right side there is a panel called "Pages" using which you can create pages for website like "Home", "About Us", "Gallery", "Products" and so on. WYSIWYG software generally also allows user to create website navigation links, as most websites have these. It is important to know that, what WYSIWYG software really does is that it generates HTML and CSS from the visual webpages you create using by drag and drop feature of WYSIWYG software. This means that your website would be technically same as if you had coded it yourself using HTML and CSS – your website will be searchable in search engines! WYSIWYG software also allows you to add keywords for search engines and have many other great features which you don't have to code yourself – even features like placing video or sound in website or adding some animation effects to your website.

Although creating websites with WYSIWYG software does not require the knowledge of website creation formatting languages – HTML and CSS, my advice would be that you know very basics about these languages, like how they work, what are their purpose and some code examples from them. It would be great if you know HTML, for example to add some specific functionality to your website not provided by WYSIWYG software (and WYSIWYG software allow you to insert your custom HTML or CSS code); or even easier – there are many HTML code sections on the web that you can directly copy and paste in your websites code – you just need to know very basics about HTML, which can be learned in one hour or less! There are several commercial WYSIWYG software available for creating websites. The good thing is that although technically they allow only creation of static websites, they can be also used to change some text or elements on your static website later very easily. For example, Serif Webplus allows you to save project files which contain all the website data. Using this project files, you can modify your website in any way after you create website - rearrange items, change colors, change texts... whenever you want. Which is the best WYSIWYG software? – you might ask. From my experience, I strongly advice you to buy Serif WebPlus. This is the best software I reviewed, because it has highest overall quality, has many features, supports HTML5, has offline help about every feature of the software and it is SEO (Search Engine Optimization) friendly – I tested on my website. It also allows you to insert search keywords and create sitemap.xml file for search engines to easily find and analyze your website. But there are other WYSIWYG software also, for example Xara Web Designer. Just look for WYSIWYG web design software and not HTML editor – which is different kind of software, it is designed for HTML and similar language code editing. The good thing is that you pay once for WYSIWYG software and you can create as many websites with it as you

want even when you don't have internet connection - you can just create website and later upload to server; this is not the case with online website builder websites, in which case you pay monthly for their service.
However, if you choose this method, you will need to spend some money on the following: domain name (about 15$/year), hosting (about 4$/month), WYSIWYG software (Serif Webplus X8 for example costs 120$ at this time of writing).
To conclude, using WYSIWYG software is a very good and easy option for creating beautiful, professional static websites in short amount of time.

Creating websites using online website builder websites

This is newer way of creating static websites compared to other methods: there are some websites/companies that allow you to create website using other websites specifically designed for creating static websites. These websites are essentially online website editors but they are also websites themselves. The good thing about them is that you do everything online – using these website builder websites you can create your websites from any computer without the need to install any software; also, you won't loose any files and you won't need to make any backups – all your files will be created online. These website builder websites are mostly for

people who have very few technical knowledge, because they are very easy to use: you just need to login and build your website visually by dragging and dropping pre made buttons, text boxes etc. (this is the easiest way to create websites from all the methods discussed in the book but not the best in my opinion, as I will later explain). Users of these website builder websites don't need to know about hosting technicalities, like how to upload website using FTP and such. For these reason, companies that offer this kind of services cost more per month. On the other hand, learning about hosting is quite easy and it happens once; then, you can have more control of your website – you can manually backup your complete website for secure offline storage or you can easily move your website to other hosting server/company if you want and don't like current hosting service.
There are several such online website creation services online. One of the most popular and my recommendation is Weebly available at website www.weebly.com. Weebly is very easy to use; it also allows you to create free website but with .weebly.com ending as an address, for example your web address could be www.mysite.weebly.com. Weebly also allows you to create website with your own custom web address at .com domain, but they generally have higher prices because of simplicity. I tried to create free website with Weebly and it looked

quite professional and worked well; also, it had quite good SEO functionality even though it was built as free website. With Weebly and similar services you can create websites in hours – even without any knowledge of HTML or CSS although I would recommend learning basics of these technologies at minimum. There are other similar services also, for example Wix at website www.wix.com which is also quite good alternative to Weebly.

The drawbacks of such services is that they cost more per month (that is logical because they help you to not worry about technically building websites or about technicalities of hosting and domain) compared to companies that offer only hosting services, and that there is possibility (very low, but still) that these companies will close someday – and all your website and files are destroyed or your website will not be available, which is also very bad for your business. Also, because of they offer domains and these domains are interconnected with hosting they offer, you are limited in selecting different companies for domain names and different companies for hosting services, which I don't like; you can save some money if you can rent hosting and register domain on your own. Another disadvantage of these services is that they offer only static website creation – you can't use advantages of really dynamic websites such as content specific ads or related posts feature etc. To really understand how online website builder websites look and how they allow you to create website look at the image below (image is captured on weebly.com - online website creator website).

image 6: Screenshot of weebly.com website creator website

This is how you create websites: by dragging and dropping different kinds of website elements from the left pane - as needed. You can also create and edit website pages and select different themes for website from the top panel as you can see. Here's an image of weebly.com pricing page:

image 7: Weebly.com pricing page

As you can see, "Starter" plan is $8.00 per month, but note that you can pay only about 4$ per month if you choose to host your website by separate hosting company, like justhost.com or bluehost.com.

Creating websites using CMS engines like WordPress

CMS is short for “Content Management System”. CMS is a type of website which’s design is not interconnected with website content; design can be changed independently from content: individual pages, texts, images and navigation buttons and other static objects on website can be stayed intact while you can change overall design of complete website, like color palette, placement of different website objects (ads, banners, text...) etc. CMS engine can be used to create any kind of website you wish - from static websites to fully dynamic content generation (dynamically generating content and banners, ads, etc.) website. Using CMS engines to build websites is very popular method of creating websites today, and it has many great features; the most notable feature being the ability to create fully dynamic websites even without coding experience! CMS engines are fully programmed using PHP, so they can have any dynamic feature you might want. If you needed to code CMS website yourself, it would be very time consuming and almost impossible because of resources and knowledge of web technologies it needs to be created. You would need to know PHP, MySQL, databases, HTML, CSS and even other technologies! In fact, those who create custom CMS engines are complete group of programmers working quite long to create these engines, and they also constantly update and improve these CMS engines. But there is a very good news for you – many CMS engines are free and most importantly – most popular CMS engine in the world – WordPress is also free! About 20% of world's websites is built using WordPress because of it's simplicity, performance, security and quality!

Statistically, CMS engines are very popular technology for building websites; that's because companies can save hundreds of dollars if they create company websites using free CMS engines instead of paying thousands to web design studios to create custom website by coding from scratch. Other popular free CMS engines are Joomla and Drupal. However, there are commercial CMS engines also available, which are quite powerful, but I strongly advice you to create your website using free CMS engine WordPress - simply because it's most popular in the world and probably most powerful.

This is probably the best way to select if you want to create websites with modifiable content. CMS websites typically allow you to create “posts”, which are essentially individual pages of website. These posts can stay the same or you can change them at any time. Also, you can modify the overall design of website using themes, which are available either as free or commercial (about 50$ each). Each theme has it's unique features like pre made banner places, pre made widgets (which are like panels which can display different content like popular posts), and many other features. Another great advantage of CMS websites is that they have plugins which are addons for adding specific functionalities to websites. You can learn, for example WordPress basics in quite short time, and the great thing is that you even don’t need to know coding languages to build websites with CMS engines like WordPress. Many people just don’t know that professional, high quality websites can be created using free CMS engines, so they think that website creation is something they can never do, and they need to order web design company to make their website. That is waste of hundreds of dollars and time! You can create fully dynamic and professionally looking dynamic website! This even can not be imagined in the past - because creating dynamic website requires huge amount of time and resources - often done by group of programmers and web designers. And the last great thing about CMS engines: they allow you to install CMS engines on your own web hosting! That's great: you have complete control of your website – you can backup all your website files or you can change, remove or add any files on your hosting disk space.

However, if you choose this method, you will need to spend some money on the following: domain name (about 15$/year), hosting (about 4$/month) and some professional looking commercial theme (about 50$). On the following image you can see how WordPress admin panel looks like. From this panel you can create your website - add or edit pages, add or edit images, activate, install or deactivate plugins (which add specific functionality to WordPress website) and so on.

image 8: WordPress admin page

Creating personal blogs and websites for completely free

Sometimes we don't want to create professional corporate or company website. Sometimes we just want to create personal websites where we can write about our thoughts, ideas, stories and so on. For this kind of task it is best to create personal blog. You can create personal blog for completely free using wordpress.com (wordpress has two modes: either you can use it as CMS engine as discussed earlier or you can use it to create free website with .wordpress.com ending with free hosting) or blogger.com. These are world's most popular free blog creation websites. I recommend wordpress.com because it is the most popular in the world and it's very easy to use. Website created using these free blog creators (blogs are really just personal websites which include posts or stories in chronological order) are very search friendly - this is great for you because you don't care to make them easily searchable - this is done for you automatically, which is not the case if you would create your website yourself - you would need to insert special keywords for making it search friendly for search engines like Google and Yahoo. Another way you can use to create free website is to use weebly.com online free website creator - but your website will have .weebly.com ending and you will have limited features in free version; but you can upgrade to premium paid version to have custom domain name and more features; but generally, creating website using weebly.com and similar websites like wix.com are good in case you want to create fixed static website. If you want to create free and easy to update website you would better go with wordpress.com - you can add as many posts as you wish for free whenever you want to your wordpress blog, which is not the case with static websites created with weebly.com or similar websites.

What to learn to spend minimum amount of time and resources to create websites
My advice is that first you learn about very basics of HTML, CSS, PHP, Javascript and hosting, like what they are, how they work and how to insert custom HTML into your website; there might be case when you'll need to do this, or just learn them to understand at the very basic level how websites work. Also, it would be good if you learn about from which files website is composed (.html, image and other files), how these files are linked together and how to upload your complete website using FTP (File Transfer Protocol). Again, you don't need to know all the feature of mentioned technologies, but you just need to know very basics to understand how website works. Then, you can very easily create websites using WYSIWYG software, CMS engine or online website builder website, as previously discussed in the book. I recommend creating with

WordPress CMS engine, because it can create both static and dynamic, beautiful, technically professional websites.

Chapter 8: Meta With Seo Tags

Usage of Meta with SEO Tags

These <meta> tags will improve the SEO for the page as it describes your page in such way that search engine understand and learn about your page.

<meta> tags are one of the most important tag that will help to boost your page SEO.

Two most important things you define in the <meta> tags are keywords and description.

keywords will help to tell search engine to show your page when these keywords are searched in the search engine.

description is the small description about your page that search engine will use.

robots attribute helps to communicate with the search engine bots. You can ask robots to ignore the page to index and follow further on this page.

TAG: <meta>

ELEMENT:

<meta name="robots" content="index, follow">

<meta name="Description" CONTENT="Author: A.N. Author, Illustrator: P. Picture, Category: Books, Price: £9.24, Length: 784 pages">

<meta name="keywords" content="html5, learning, wpbootcamp, web">

<meta> tags are not displayed on the browser so you won't see anything on the page. Sample Example

<!DOCTYPE html>

```
<html>
<head>
<meta name="robots" content="index,follow">
<meta name="Description" CONTENT="Author: A.N. Author, Illustrator: P. Picture, Category: Books, Price: £9.24, Length: 784 pages">
<meta name="keywords" content="html5, learning, techiesbootcamp, web">
<title>META tags - Search Engine Optimization</title>
</head>
<body>
<!-
Meta tags that Google understands

https://support.google.com/webmasters/answer
/79812?hl=en
-->
<h1>Invisible Tags</h1>
</body>
</html> LIVE PREVIEW
```

9.2 – Meta tags with View Port

Usage of Meta with View Port

View ports are used to tell browsers how to scale (zoom) the page on the browser.

Things like:

- Width and Height
- Scaling (Zoom)

TAG:

<meta>

ELEMENT:

```
<meta charset="utf8">
<meta name="viewport" content="width=device-width, initialscale=1.0">
```

charset="utf8" tells the browser that HTML content is written in that character set. We have different character set for different languages. Like we have SHIFTJIS to represent the Japanese character.

How to see the ViewPort Settings:

Press CTRL + SHIFT + I button to bring the inspect window and click on the "Toggle Device Toolbar" -> Change the Layout to Responsive – 400 x 300 size.

Sample Example:

```
<!DOCTYPE html>
<html>
<head>
<meta charset="utf-8">
<meta name="viewport" content="width=device-width, initial-scale=1.0">
<meta name="robots" content="index,follow">
<meta name="Description" CONTENT="Author: A.N. Author, Illustrator: P. Picture, Category: Books, Price: £9.24, Length: 784 pages">
<meta name="keywords" content="html5, learning, wpbootcamp, web">
<title>With Viewport Tag</title>
</head>
<body>
<h1>With Viewport</h1>
```

```
<img src ="dog1.jpg" alt="German Shepherd">
<p>The German Shepherd (German: Deutscher Schäferhund, German pronunciation: is a breed of medium to large-sized working dog that originated in Germany. The breed's officially recognized name is German Shepherd Dog in the English language (sometimes abbreviated as GSD). The breed was once known as the Alsatian in Britain and Ireland.[5] The German Shepherd is a relatively new breed of dog, with their origin dating to 1899. As part of the Herding Group, German Shepherds are working dogs developed originally for herding sheep. </p>
</body>
</html>
```

LIVE PREVIEW

Exercise 1

DOWNLOAD THE EXERCISE 1

Exercise 1: Change the Viewport initial-scale=5.0 and observe the output in the inspect window. LIVE PREVIEW

9.3 – Meta tags without View Port

Usage of Meta without View Port

If you disable the viewport then the page is not scaled to match the device size.

How to see the ViewPort Settings:

Press CTRL + SHIFT + I button to bring the inspect window and click on the "Toggle Device Toolbar" -> Change the Layout to Responsive – 400 x 300 size. LIVE PREVIEW

9.5 – Page Auto Redirect

Usage of Page Auto Redirect

With the <meta> tag you can tell browser to redirect the page to another page after n number of seconds.

This is very much useful when you want to show an ads for 5 seconds and auto redirect to the home page.

You will find site like forbes.com does it by showing an Quote for the day + ads for 5 seconds and then route to the main page.

TAG: <meta>

ELEMENT:

```
<meta http-equiv=”refresh” content=”10; url=https://wpfreelancer.com/”>
```

url indicate which site the page should redirect to

Sample Example:

To see the page redirect go to Inspect mode (CTRL + SHIFT + I) -> Click on Network and observe the refresh.

```
<!DOCTYPE html>
<html>
<head>
<meta charset="utf-8">
<meta name="viewport" content="width=device-width, initial-scale=1.0">
<meta name="robots" content="index,follow">
```

<meta name="description" CONTENT="Author: A.N. Author, Illustrator: P. Picture, Category: Books, Price: £9.24, Length: 784 pages">
<meta name="keywords" content="html5, learning, wpbootcamp, web">
<title>Auto Redirect to WPFreelancer.com</title> <meta http-equiv="refresh" content="10; url=https://wpfreelancer.com/">
</head> <body>
<h1>Page redirect to WPFreelancer.com after 10 Sec...</h1>
<img src ="dog1.jpg" alt="German Shepherd">
<p>The German Shepherd (German: Deutscher Schäferhund, German pronunciation: is a breed of medium to large-sized working dog that originated in Germany. The breed's officially recognized name is German Shepherd Dog in the English language (sometimes abbreviated as GSD). The breed was once known as the Alsatian in Britain and Ireland.[5] The German Shepherd is a relatively new breed of dog, with their origin dating to 1899. As part of the Herding Group, German Shepherds are working dogs developed originally for herding sheep. </p>
</body> </html>
Live Preview
10. LAYOUTS

10 LAYOUTS
Layout of Page

In this section, you will learn basics HTML elements that are used to make a HTML page. This is a pseudo code that you can apply for all the page as a structure.

Even though the layout of the page differs from site to site but the basics tags that makes up the layout does not differ.

Layout of the page are made of:

1. Header – <header></header>
2. Navigation – <nav></nav>
3. Side Bars – <aside></aside>
4. Content
5. Sections – <section></section>
6. Articles – <article></article>
7. Footer – <footer></footer>

HTML has the tags to represent each of the item and you can use them to draw a basic structure of the page.

10.1 – Layout 1

Simple HTML Layout

This simple HTML page layout will include all the tags that is used to create a simple layout.

HTML page layout is divided into the following sections.

TAG: <header>, <nav>, <aside>, <section>, <article> and <footer>

ELEMENT:

<body>

<header>Heading</header>

<nav>Navigation</nav>

```
<aside>Navigation</aside>
<section>
<article>Content</article>
</section>
<footer>Footer</footer>
```

Sample Example:

```
<!DOCTYPE html>
<html>
<head>
<title>Sample HTML5 Layout</title>
</head>
<body>
<header>
<h1>Page Layout 1</h1>
</header>
<hr>
<section> <article>
<header><h1><u>Article 1</u></h1></header>
<p>Lorem Ipsum is simply dummy text of the
printing and typesetting industry. Lorem Ipsum
has been the industry's standard dummy text
ever since the 1500s, when an unknown printer
took a galley of type and scrambled it to make a
type specimen book.</p>
<p>#End of Article 1</p>
</article>
<article>
<header><h1><u>Article 2</u></h1></header>
<p>Lorem Ipsum is simply dummy text of the
printing and typesetting industry. Lorem Ipsum
```

has been the industry's standard dummy text ever since the 1500s, when an unknown printer took a galley of type and scrambled it to make a type specimen book.</p>
<p>#End of Article 2</p>
</article>
</section>
<footer>
<hr>
Copyright (C) 2018. WPbootcamp.com
</footer>
</body> </html>

LIVE PREVIEW
Exercise 1
DOWNLOAD THE EXERCISE 1
Exercise 1: Create an About Page and Contact Page and link the pages from
the home page.
LIVE PREVIEW
11. ADDITIONAL TAGS

11 ADDITIONAL TAGS
Additional Tags

www.ingramcontent.com/pod-product-compliance
Lightning Source LLC
Chambersburg PA
CBHW071123050326
40690CB00008B/1320

9781774857861